Town&Country

Elegant Entertaining

Francine Maroukian

A FAIR STREET / WELCOME BOOK

HEARST BOOKS

A DIVISION OF STERLING PUBLISHING CO., INC.

NEW YORK

Contents

Foreword

THIS IS THE SECOND BOOK we've published about elegant living. Our first, *Town & Country Elegant Weddings*, was a natural first effort for us. Ever since the magazine's inception in 1846, *Town & Country* (then called *The Home Journal*) has covered news about who was marrying whom. People cared about those things back in the mid-nineteenth century and, amazingly, they still do, even at the beginning of the twenty-first.

Our next subject for a book was as easy a choice for us as was weddings. It would have to be about another subject dear to our hearts and about which we know a good deal: entertaining—primarily at home but also in restaurants. While the national trend in America these days seems to be cook less and dine out

more, I have found this to be far less true among our readers, whose homes are their sanctuaries—places of pride, to be shared with friends and family, for special occasions and for no special reason at all.

Whoever would be the author of this book had to possess several qualities: be a proficient cook; know how to give a successful dinner party; be able to write to the high standards of the magazine; and, finally, to understand and embrace the *Town & Country* reader. We found all this and more in Francine Maroukian, who has been a cook and a caterer for many years and has lately turned her considerable talents to writing. What I didn't expect—and what came as a bonus—was Francine's clever approach to the book and her total absorption in the subject. I should have known better.

Francine and I met in 1985, when she catered an open house for a good friend of mine around the Christmas holidays. I was so impressed by her relaxed manner and tasty food that I asked her to handle a dinner party at my apartment the following January. I recently came across the menu, which was relatively simple but so good. To start: smoked salmon with sweet brown bread and herbed cheese; small pizzas topped with black olive paste (olivada) and smoked mozzarella cheese. For the main course: a winter veal stew served with spinach, new potatoes, zucchini, and peppers. That was followed by a green salad served with chevre. Dessert was a warm apple crisp with ice cream. If it sounds homey and delicious, let me assure you that it was. I chose the wine—a 1979 Ducru-Beaucaillou—and took care of the table setting. It was, as I recall, a wonderful evening.

One dinner party led to another and then another, to the point where Francine became the only caterer I wanted in my kitchen, partly because she was so good at what she did and partly because I simply loved having her around. She always had a great crew working with her and was so funny and irreverent that my husband and I would find ourselves drawn to the kitchen in between our duties as host and hostess. It was a dark day in our lives when Francine announced in 1998 that that Christmas's open house would be her last official catering job. She would be devoting her time thereafter to only one of her passions (and, believe me, she has plenty) and write for a living.

But I was not about to let Francine slip away so easily. She was the first person I thought of to write this book, and she took it on with all the verve that envelops everything in her life—wholeheartedly, completely, unqualifiedly. The result is a highly readable—entertaining, if you will—book on elegant entertaining.

When I use the word "elegant," I do not mean stiff or pretentious or formal (although we address the subject of formal entertaining within these pages). There is, to me, nothing deadlier at a dinner party than an air of pomposity. It puts everybody on edge. Unless you are royalty or as close to that as one comes in America, don't even think about it. By elegant, I mean setting a beautiful table, adding personal touches that are yours alone, and inviting guests who will add charm and warmth to the occasion.

Entertaining with elegance extends beyond the dining room (if you even have one; many people these days prefer an open eat-in area). Indeed, it begins as your guests step through the doorway. How quickly will they be greeted and made to feel comfortable? If other guests have preceded them, how soon will they be introduced and engaged in conversation? Elegance includes everything, from the lighting in the foyer to the flowers placed throughout the house. It means arranging intimate seating areas and making your guests feel as important when they leave your home as they were when they first arrived.

All of this requires a great deal from the host, and, in all my years of giving parties—many of which I have done on my own, without the services of an outside caterer—I have never once underestimated the amount of forethought and organization parties take. Nobody just "throws" a party without a great deal of planning and care. If they do, it will feel exactly that—thrown together. If entertaining were a cinch, I'd be doing it every night. So why do it at all, if there are so many details and so much preparation? Because one of the most generous and gracious gestures you can make for people you like is to open your home—and in a real sense, yourself—to them.

Entertaining is a gift, just as I hope this book will be for those you care about.

Pamela Fiori
Editor-in-Chief, *Town & Country*

Introduction

I F EVER A PERSONAL PHILOSOPHY radiated universal truth and made a world of common sense, it is the late Elsie de Wolfe's straightforward interpretation of good taste as: Suitability! Suitability! Suitability! Miss de Wolfe, America's first female professional interior decorator (credited with popularizing everything from parquet floors to chintz-covered sofas), may have been talking about design, but her practical credo goes to the heart of home entertaining: A successful party is the one that is right for you, for your home and for your guests.

Although the best parties often have a warm, spontaneous feel, that doesn't mean they happen by chance. Before you lift a finger or a telephone, select a napkin or a flower, it is essential to spend time thinking about the atmosphere you want to create. What are your entertaining expectations and needs for this particular party? If conversation is your priority and you picture your guests congregated around the dining room table engrossed in conversation, then a seated party is your best choice. If you want to give your guests the freedom to mix on their own, serving a buffet-style meal will encourage people to group and regroup in an informal and spontaneous manner. When variety (in both people and food) ranks as number one on your party agenda, and you envision a hodgepodge of guests mingling against a backdrop of twinkling lights and tinkling ice cubes, give a classic cocktail party.

And if you're a "more is merrier" host who subscribes to the theory that a party's only limitations are dictated by the local fire law, it is time to gather everyone together for an old-fashioned holiday open house.

Deciding to entertain outdoors brings its own set of special considerations, but the right deck or terrace adds infinite party possibilities, from seated luncheons to sunset cocktail buffets. Still, there may be times when your home (inside or out) is not the best setting for your party. Perhaps you are in the middle of a renovation, or just want to add another dimension to the usual seated dinner. When the situation calls for it, restaurants can be used like an extension of your dining room, fulfilling the role once played by private clubs, offering made-to-order ambience and the culinary range of a professional kitchen.

No matter where or when your party is taking place, any entertaining you do should bear your own mark. If a party calls for professional help (even if you have developed a working relationship with a caterer), your involvement is still vital in making decisions about everything from the aesthetic considerations (flowers, lighting, music) to the practical concerns (where to put all the coats). Developing, maintaining, and communicating personal style is paramount. While each party style may embody certain basic rules, they are not there to be followed blindly. They are only guideposts on the road to the care and feeding and comfort of you and your guests.

CHAPTER 1
The Seated Dinner

ALTHOUGH THE IMAGE of perfectly attired dinner guests gathered around a grand table remains indelibly fixed in our minds as the archetypal seated party, how we get our guests to that table, and what we serve them, reflect our changing times. In the 1993 screen adaptation of Edith Wharton's masterpiece of manners *The Age of Innocence*, director Martin Scorsese re-creates a world fettered by Victorian convention: "What can you expect of a girl who was allowed to wear black satin to her coming out party?" sniffs a prim society wife. In this world, where social position dictated a party's guest list and conformity to tradition dominated everything else, a dinner party was considered to be "at best no light matter." With a sweeping overhead view of a majestic table, lavishly set, with course after course of complicated culinary arrangements on gilded Sèvres porcelain, Scorsese's film gives us a dramatic look into this ceremonial realm, when entertaining

Whatever the occasion— from formal to casual, an intimate family gathering or a full scale celebration—the seated party remains a favorite way to entertain.

meant navigating a labyrinth of preordained rules and enjoyment was forced to take a backseat to etiquette.

In these modern times, such formal dinners are primarily reserved for galas and affairs of state, rarely occurring in a home setting. Instead, today's hosts and hostesses have the freedom to combine the old with the new; they view the seated party as an occasion to create their own entertaining style. Whether they work in bold saturated colors or pale subdued palettes, choose the coziness of a homespun look or favor more exotic elements, setting the table has become an art of personal

Form and Function

We may be past Edith Wharton's "age of innocence," but the custom of using specific standards to determine levels of formality in seated parties has endured. It is impossible to pigeonhole every party, but three general types remain: informal, semiformal, and formal. Although these words do not appear on the invitation, the implied level of formality helps to define every aspect of the party, from the way the invitation is issued to the setting and service.

The Informal Dinner

- Invitations are issued over the telephone or in person, often with only a few days' notice.
- The party starts on the early side, between six-thirty and seven-thirty.
- Table settings are simple, often without decoration or candles.
- Seating is assigned by the host or hostess, without place cards.
- There are never more than three courses.
- Service may or may not be handled by staff. In some cases, the meal is served "family style."
- After the meal, coffee is served at the table.

The Semiformal Dinner

- Invitations may be issued through the mail or over the telephone with two to four weeks' notice, followed with a written reminder two weeks before the party.
- Guests generally arrive between seven-thirty and eight.
- The table setting includes linens (runners, tablecloth, or place mats), table decorations, and candles.
- Seating may be assigned by place card, but with first names only, and there may be a handwritten menu card.
- There are at least four courses.
- Staff handles service.
- Guests usually adjourn to another room for coffee.

The Formal Dinner

- Engraved invitations, worded in the third person, are sent with four weeks' notice and are acknowledged in writing within two days of receipt.
- Guests arrive at eight or eight-thirty, and dinner is served forty-five minutes to an hour later.
- There are rarely fewer than twelve guests.
- The table is set with white or cream-colored linens, centerpieces, and light-colored candles.
- Place cards are used. These have full names and titles (the same way the person would be introduced, such as Senator or Doctor) and can be handwritten or, on the most formal occasions, engraved.
- Menu cards (with accompanying wines) are used and are typically in French. These can be handwritten in script or, for the most elaborate occasions, engraved.
- There are a minimum of five courses.
- Service is formal, with one butler for every six to eight guests.
- There is no coffee service at the table. Due to the length of the meal, the host will move the party into another room, giving guests an opportunity to converse with a number of other guests.

To a lesser extent, these entertaining standards are also applied to luncheons, which generally fall into two general categories: casual (or informal) and more elaborate (think of this as informal with extras). In either case, the meal is shorter than dinner (two, at the most three, courses) and the table is simply set, with place mats (or runners) instead of linens. Although there may be some sort of table decoration, candles are never used during the day.

Luncheon and/or brunch invitations, issued verbally or through the mail, call for guests to arrive no more than thirty minutes before the meal is served. Wine or a cocktail may be offered but rarely will there be passed hors d'oeuvre.

expression. For example, a table setting may include a formal touch like menu cards while incorporating the patterned linens usually reserved for more casual dining. In other words, you may use the family silver, but you do not have to give your parents' dinner party. Adherence to rigid standards of perfection is no longer required or even *en vogue*. As the ever pragmatic tastemaker Elsie de Wolfe once warned, "It is not chic to be too chic."

Getting Personal

SUZANNE WILLIAMSON AND PETER POLLAK

EVERYTHING YOU'VE HEARD about Southern hospitality is true—at least in the Beaufort, South Carolina, home of Suzanne Williamson and her husband, Peter Pollak. Suzanne, an author and lecturer on home and business entertaining, is living proof that those who teach can also do . . . and do with passion. "I would rather give a party than go to one," says Suzanne. For this hostess, it all starts with the invitations, and she believes that a telephone call is the best way to involve her guests. It's like advance public relations, she explains. "Guests become excited about the party by the sound of your voice. 'I can't wait for you to meet so-and-so,' I tell them. Or, 'I'm making your favorite dish.' Not only do I get a response right away, but people think they're going to have the best time. And when they get there, they do."

She plans her guest list by inviting people who give her "a good feeling" and believes that odd numbers are more interesting than even numbers, as in a flower arrangement. According to Suzanne, seven is the maximum number that can participate easily in the same conversation. Exceed that limit, and your guests will talk to the person on their right or their left. "And when there are two, three, or four conversations going on, you might miss out on the best one," she says. "An odd number of people gives you the chance to show your heart. All of us know single, widowed, and divorced people who are often left out," she remarks. "But that one extra person can be the guest who makes your party unforgettable."

Suzanne's habit of greeting guests personally and offering a big hug as soon as they walk in the door makes them feel welcome immediately. When first-time guest

A party starts at the front door, where Suzanne Williamson believes that greeting guests herself is the best kind of welcome.

17

Suzanne graciously makes the leap from the kitchen (above) to the head of the table (opposite).

Pat Conroy arrived early, Suzanne couldn't entertain the novelist and finish the pasta dough she was making, so she greeted him warmly—and put him right to work. "He learned how to make pasta that night and was so happy about it that he telephoned the next day to ask if I would write a cookbook with him," she recalls. "Welcoming my guest at the door started my new career."

The whole point of a party is to make people as comfortable as possible, says the hostess. As guests arrive, Peter concentrates on the bar while Suzanne solidifies her seating plan. "A good guest is someone who takes part, either by listening or entertaining others," she says, "and so I start by sprinkling in the best entertainers around the table and filling in with everyone else." She knows where she wants everyone, and usually directs guests to their seats herself. "I only use place cards if I'm having a big group," she says. "Then there's less confusion when it comes time to sit down." She sets her big, round table, an American piece dating to 1760, with antique linen place mats—on holidays she'll always use a tablecloth. ("I don't know why; certain things just seem proper to me.") She stays away from formal centerpieces, preferring a line of candles down the center of the table and whatever fruits and vegetables might be in season: lemons, eggplants, artichokes, even spring onions bunched in small tureens.

Suzanne is one hostess who loves cooking for her own dinner parties, including the homemade soups, pastas, and breads she serves. Although she usually runs out of the time needed to make hors d'oeuvre, that's all right with her. "I don't really like them," she confesses. "Plus I want people to have a big appetite for dinner." And since she believes that two desserts are better than one, she tries to make a little something extra, like truffles or cookies, to go with coffee. Moving people gracefully from cocktails to dinner always takes longer than you think, she points out.

Suzanne Williamson's
Never-Fail Dinner Menu

Roast Chicken
Crispy Sautéed Potatoes
Spinach with Garlic
Olive Oil Rolls
Chocolate Tart
Grapefruit Rind Truffles
Coffee and Tea

"That's why a dessert soufflé is a better choice than a first-course soufflé. You don't want to rush your guests just to accommodate your menu."

And if you don't have Suzanne's enthusiasm or experience in the kitchen? Everybody has something they're good at, she counters. "If flowers are your thing, concentrate on flowers. If it's cooking, then that's where you should put your energy." When it comes to planning a menu, Suzanne states her preference: impressive and easy. "I find that roasts are always a success—a roast chicken, beef tenderloin, or loin of pork. Most people love these down-home main courses."

The Menu

The perfect plate is a balanced mix of flavors, colors, and textures.

Unlike a meal served from a buffet (where guests choose from a variety of dishes), the menu at a seated party is predetermined by the hostess—trickier than you might think.

Although most people understand that party food should fit the occasion (there is a time and place for filet and foie gras, and brunch in August is not it), many other considerations go into shaping a menu for a seated dinner.

The menu ménage à trois: *crispy, crunchy, creamy*

A menu should always be balanced with respect to color and flavor, but the most important element to consider is texture. For example, a meal that starts with vichyssoise, continues with rack of lamb, mashed potatoes, and vegetable purée, then ends with velvety chocolate mousse for dessert is too consistently thick and rich—it needs a little snap and crunch. Consider the same rack of lamb paired with oven-roasted potatoes and *haricots verts* tossed with toasted walnuts, preceded by slivers of Asian greens floating in a thin broth and followed by a lemon tart for dessert. This menu works because it is not monotonous. Flavors, colors, and textures rotate throughout, with course-by-course contrasts.

20

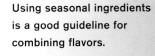

Using seasonal ingredients
is a good guideline for
combining flavors.

Mixing and matching

When it comes to texture, diversity is the key, so it helps to view the entire meal as a progression of courses, with one kind of texture following another. Start by framing your menu around a specific dish: the main course or whatever you consider to be the pièce de résistance (like the pumpkin ravioli first course everyone raves about, or the fabulous crème brûlée that your guest of honor adores). Then back into the other courses, making selections based on the dominant texture of that one dish you just have to have. To avoid duplication of textures and flavors, decide on hors d'oeuvre after all the other courses have been determined.

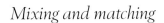

However, considering the choices food markets now offer, there ought to be some kind of relationship among the courses: a unifying thread that runs through the menu without duplicating ingredients. You can never go wrong with nature. Using seasonal ingredients as a guideline for putting dishes together makes good food sense. For example, if you're serving lobster in July, a strawberry tart is a better fit for dessert than apple crisp.

Food fantasies

No matter how uninhibited you may be about food, your guests might not share your experimental palate, and parties are not the place to show your epicurean bravado. Even the most creative chefs confine their more unusual pairings to *amuse-bouches* that offer just a tiny, startling taste before the meal. Instead, rely on little twists to transform the simplest dish into something complex. Give your guests the chance to be adventurous with a rich cream sauce or quirky salsa served on the side.

Classics, not clichés

There's no reason to bowl people over with food, even on special occasions. Even people with the most sophisticated palates appreciate simple food when it is beautifully prepared, and there will always be a certain graciousness in serving classic dishes. Your main-course repertoire can be small—even successful caterers choose from a limited number of favorites, accessorized with different side dishes according to the time of year. The same roast chicken that works with root vegetables and potato gratin in the fall can be served with sliced fresh tomatoes and sugar snap peas come summer.

The Original Dinner Theater

EVELYN AND LEONARD LAUDER

IF ALL THE WORLD'S A STAGE, Evelyn and Leonard Lauder's parties in their New York home are front and center. For Evelyn, senior corporate vice president at Estée Lauder Companies and an accomplished photographer, "parties are theater," and as with any good director, her approach is both cerebral and artistic. Parties are more successful when you think them through and coordinate all the aspects," she explains.

The first step is to determine the reason for the party, and Evelyn is quick to point out that "just spending time with friends" qualifies. "Once you have established your reason, the next step is to carefully choose your guests in relation to that specific occasion and to each other," Evelyn says, expanding on her big-picture view. "For your party to 'hang together,' you must be very thoughtful about whom to invite. Even if you want to bring different groups together, you can't just choose from a disjointed list." It is the custom of many experienced hostesses to treat their guest list like a wish list, and Evelyn is no exception. She structures her guest list around key people, makes sure they are available, and then clusters other guests around her core group. She issues invitations "every way imaginable." She may e-mail or telephone with an immediate "hold the date," but always follows up with an invitation or written reminder as a courtesy to those with busy social calendars. Since Evelyn's seating plan depends on her guest list, she stays "up to date" and "up to the minute" with responses, especially for larger gatherings. "There is one master list that controls everything," she says. "It's almost biblical."

Like most theater lovers who enjoying chronicling each performance, she maintains her own party archives by asking everyone to sign a guest book. Keeping one is a great way to relive the parties, she explains, and provides a useful record of who has been there, and with whom. "Then I can turn to someone and say 'Oh, you know so-and-so. You met at my house ten years ago,'" she says. Even if people don't sign a book, Evelyn insists on preserving some kind of guest diary. One year when hosting a benefit for the Whitney Museum, she had all the guests—a who's who of the American art world, from Andy Warhol to Jasper Johns—autograph an exhibit poster.

Evelyn Lauder uses her photographer's eye to create artistic and individualistic table settings.

Both Evelyn and Leonard make a point of greeting their guests personally at the door, with staff members stationed nearby holding trays with prepoured glasses of water, white wine, and champagne. "This was something I saw when we went to the White House, and I just loved the idea," Evelyn recalls. "It's so welcoming." Although cocktails from a full bar are also available, being able to get a drink immediately upon entering not only makes people feel like they're "already at the party," it also speeds up service at larger gatherings.

Evelyn's solution to the problem of seating large parties fell unexpectedly into her lap at her hairdresser's, where she noticed a woman using the ideal tool to seat a thousand people at a party at Lincoln Center: a binder of classroom attendance charts. Their neat system of chair assignments (pockets and name cards) made the charts perfectly suited to table seating, with each classroom row representing a table of ten. "I knew this was the answer to my prayers," recalls Evelyn. "It's so simple, and I love the flexibility of working with cards." Seats can be assigned and reassigned easily, and if she's seating four or five tables, she merely shuffles the cards until she gets exactly the configurations she wants.

When it comes to the table, Evelyn plans her menus and settings simultaneously, often creating themes for parties. On occasion, when she uses a Japanese caterer who provides kimono-clad waitresses, she sets the table with beautiful chopsticks and Japanese-style flower arrangements. Or she might create a party theme around an experience that she and the guests have shared. Describing a reunion for the group with whom she traveled to South America, she recalls that whenever they flew over the mountains (which they did in a helicopter), she always commented that the bunched tree tops looked like broccoli. For her party, Evelyn decorated the table with broccoli and tucked each place card into the propeller of a little toy helicopter.

When there are more than three courses, Evelyn adds a menu card to each place setting. "It's only fair to let guests know how to pace themselves," she explains. If there is a guest of honor, the menu card is inscribed with that person's name and the date of the party, to serve as a memento.

Evelyn, who has given hundreds of parties and entertained thousands of people, admits she has developed her flair for entertaining over the years by "taking bits and pieces from other people's parties." She gives the same practical advice to anyone interested in perfecting entertaining skills: see how other people entertain, take the best and use it yourself.

The Seating

WHAT GOES AROUND COMES AROUND

SCANDAL, MURDER, AND SEATING CHARTS might seem like an unlikely mix, but they add up to a fascinating theme in many of best-selling author Dominick Dunne's books. Dunne, who has graced many a gold ballroom chair in his own life, writes about crime. But it is high-society crime, and there is usually one delicious plot-thickening moment when a blue-blooded socialite finds herself sharing dinner and confidences with some blackballed scoundrel. In this complicated world of power, privilege, and ruined reputations, seating can make or break a party. "Maisie Verdun has a genius for seating," says one of Dunne's characters in *People Like Us*. "She agonizes over her placement."

Perhaps your seating chart won't create quite the same social drama, or have the same far-fetching consequences, but it is still important to create a strategy for seating your guests.

For entertaining guru Lee Bailey, the best seating starts with a round table. "You can squeeze in more people at a round table than a rectangle would accommodate, creating a festive camaraderie," says Bailey. If you have a large rectangular or square table, he suggests changing your usual seating habits to accommodate the number of guests—grouping chairs together at one end of a large table, for example, to create an intimate atmosphere at a smaller party. "It's how you position your guests that counts," he says.

Balance your seating chart by alternating the best conversationalists and the best listeners.

Turning the Table

Once upon an entertaining time, a guest's conversational obligation extended only to immediate table partners: diners spoke right to left, or left to right. At some point during the meal, it was the host's responsibility to "turn the table" by concluding the conversation with the guest on one side and starting anew with the guest on the other. Everyone watched the host for this signal, and then, in one smooth, perfectly choreographed moment, guests made a polite about face.

Peerless Table Seating

ALICE MASON

Paying most of her attention to seating, Alice Mason insists on unfussy table decorations and fascinating dinner conversation.

WITH ALL DUE RESPECT TO ARCHIMEDES, who proclaimed, "Give me where to stand, and I will move the earth," Alice Mason, one of Manhattan's most prominent residential real estate brokers and an accomplished hostess, only needs a chair. No one seats people as well as Alice. No one.

And what people: presidents, diplomats, movie and media stars, publishing and business moguls. In the tradition of Gertrude Stein, Perle Mesta, and the other great twentieth-century "salon-keepers" whose chief entertainment was bringing together fascinating figures, Alice is a great socializer. Her approach to constructing a guest list and a seating plan is so sophisticated that it's simple. "I have a short attention span and am absolutely panicked about being bored," she says. "And about boring others. I only invite interesting people, and seat them where I think they will have the best time." If Alice has a secret, this is it: She seats eight people at a forty-two-inch round table, which creates a very intimate setting. (Since most people use a fifty-four-inch round to seat the same number of guests, you might say it's a *close* and intimate setting.) Alice believes that using such a small table allows the whole group to be in on the discussion. "I think people only want to 'talk left or right' if they're in love," explains Alice, who always appoints a host for each table (someone who knows how to get and keep the conversational ball rolling)—a distinction that is made right on his or her place card.

Alice issues her invitations over the telephone herself (no assistant, no secretary) and follows up with a custom-printed, fill-in-the-blank reminder card. You've seen custom printing; you've seen fill-in-the-blank invitations. But only a hostess with Alice

Alice's entertaining savvy combines these two elements to provide her guests with an efficient, but still personal, reminder card.

She serves cocktails at eight o'clock, dinner at nine (although it takes a half hour to seat everyone), and the evening is over by eleven-fifteen or eleven-thirty. "Once you leave the table, you leave the house," she says. The *decorations de table* are kept to a minimum: candles and perhaps a small vase of flowers. Tables filled with *objets* don't add much to the evening, she maintains—once you've seen them, you've seen them. The meal is short: three courses, no salad. And coffee is served at the table. The most important job of a host is to give the guests a good time, she says. "They won't keep coming back unless they have one."

Modern Traditionalists

TERRY AND DENNIS STANFILL

GUESTS AT THE PASADENA, CALIFORNIA, HOME of Terry Stanfill, international representative for Christie's Auction House, and her husband, Dennis, enjoy the best of all possible worlds. Years of experience entertaining at home make Terry a confident, at-ease hostess whose seamless blend of classic and contemporary sensibilities (as well as her understanding of "informal" and "formal" customs) creates a fanciful, eclectic atmosphere.

Invitations from Terry typically come via telephone, followed by a written reminder. She makes it a practice to two-time these reminders, telling guests not only when to arrive but what time she expects to serve dinner. For example, a reminder note or written invitation will read: drinks at seven-thirty, dinner at eight-fifteen. "I like to give people the chance to adjust their arrival so they're not exhausted by the time we sit down," she says.

"In my own life, I've developed a *que será, será* attitude when it comes to entertaining," she says. "I do everything I can to prepare, then sit back and let it happen."

Terry believes that seating is absolutely the most important consideration for a dinner party. While drawing up her guest lists, Terry plans ahead, thinking about who would be good together and what one guest may have to offer to another. By the time she has completed her list, she has her seating chart. Like many hosts, she avoids seating husbands and wives next to each other, "a patriarchal practice" she believes stultifies conversation.

Although she has been known to drape shimmering saris on her table for one of her larger, off-beat theme parties, Terry admits that her favorite dinner is an intimate gathering of eight to ten carefully chosen guests. The couple begin by serving a glass of champagne (ever the diplomats, the couple offers both French and California champagne) or Prosecco, a bubbly dry Italian wine. ("And certainly my husband will make someone a martini if they like," says Terry.) The accompanying hors d'oeuvre are purposely, elegantly spare: a few

homemade cheese biscuits or tiny mushroom croustades. Serving heavy hors d'oeuvre, advises the hostess, can keep guests standing around too long, not to mention that conversation is often interrupted by waiters describing what is on their trays. "I think that whole practice started when people drank much more than we do today," says Terry. "I, for one, prefer that my guests come to the table a little 'hungry.'"

Because this hostess likes people to sit down to something hot, her menus often start with a pasta dish. "I am more and more attracted to *cucina rustica*, not wanting to serve overly

Table settings for a seated party can go from the simple to the dramatic.

elaborate food in my home," she says. While she might offer something like a cannelloni of eggplant, one of her favorite first-course choices for any dinner is risotto. "For me, it's all seasonal," she says. In the autumn, she serves risotto with porcini; in the spring, risotto primavera; and in the summer, with zucchini. The menu usually includes three courses. But no salad. ("Even though we grow wonderful lettuces in our garden, I believe salad is a lunch food.")

Underlying Beauty

There is more to setting a table than meets the eye, and many hosts take the precaution of spreading an underliner (made from heavy fabric, such as felt) on the table before the tablecloth is laid. Helpful in reducing noise, this underliner is called a silence cloth. It also protects the surface of the table, bestowing a luxurious thickness and better drape to the tablecloth while preventing it from slipping. When a decorative overlay is positioned over the tablecloth, a second (slightly thinner) protective cloth can be placed between the layers to prevent spills from soaking through. This double safeguard is the reason Terry can relax when there are glasses of red wine hovering above her Fortuny cloth. "Sandwiched between the Fortuny cloth and the overlay is a waterproof flannel cloth," she explains. "Over the years, there have been very few spills—even on the top cloth. I often use old Venetian glass tumblers for wine, with solid bases instead of traditional stem glasses. Maybe that helps. *Fortuna domus*."

**Terry Stanfill makes use
of her garden for seasonal
table decorations.**

Terry's table settings are another example of her timeless, never trendy, style. Her signature look starts with a floor-length Fortuny cloth on a sixty-inch round table, at which she seats eight to ten people. The cloth is a subtle, ivory-on-ivory design in an overall pattern of small flowers centered within squares. "For versatility, I can change the color scheme with decorative overlays because the tone-on-tone design of the Fortuny fabric is so neutral," she says. Inspiration for arrangements springs from what's on hand: flowers and fruit from the garden or containers and vases that the hostess already owns. "Given the right lead time, I may be able to coax my garden into giving me exactly what I need," she says. Her favorite color combination is pale green with purple: lavender-streaked, yellow-green figs set against dark green fig leaves, or clustered blue bells and myrtle blossoms. The test of a successful arrangement? When Terry can stand back and say to herself, "I like it."

The Flowers

32

FLOWERS MAKE THEIR MOST VALUABLE CONTRIBUTION to atmosphere at seated parties when they are an integral part of table decoration. Whether you create the flower displays yourself or turn that responsibility over to a floral decorator, think twice before settling on a centerpiece "arrangement." Formal centerpieces may never go out of style, but they are often too high and too stiff (no matter how artfully constructed), sending out a message you don't really mean to give. "When I see one imposing 'arrangement' plunked dead center, flanked by tapers, I know I'm in for a serious evening," says design authority and lifestyle author Lee Bailey. "Leave that to your mother-in-law."

Instead of working up toward the ceiling, bring the floral focus down to the table. In other words, think supper club. Elsie de Wolfe, legendary arbiter of twentieth-century domestic taste, gave timeless entertaining advice when she dictated, "Plates should be hot, hot, hot; glasses cold, cold, cold; and table decorations low, low, low."

One option is the swag-style arrangement, in which flowers trail from the center of a shallow container, providing the delicate scale necessary for intimate settings. Augmenting blooms with stems of exotic greens creates a natural look and accomplishes the ultimate goal of floral design: bringing the outside in.

Another way to "go low" is by using small but tightly packed masses of flowers grouped here and there to punctuate a long table, providing spots of color and texture as well as more room when it comes time to serve. Whether you combine pale- and vividly colored stems of the same flowers (like white, blush, rose, and fuchsia peonies) or choose to cluster monochromatic bouquets (differently shaped flowers in the same tone, perhaps hydrangea and viburnum in shades of green ranging from celadon to chartreuse), rarely will you get two arrangements that are exactly alike. What you will have are flowers that mix but don't exactly match, creating a harmonious, sophisticated table landscape.

To achieve this lush look, use small containers with narrow openings; these will hold stems closely together while allowing blooms to spread. Work in height proportions of two-thirds vase and one-third flowers, cutting stems to slightly uneven lengths for a multitiered but casually elegant effect. And since stems can be the least attractive part of a flower, consider using opaque containers like mint julep cups and tumblers made from silver or pewter.

Keeping the flowers and candles low creates an intimate feeling.

33

The New Spirit of Entertaining

SYLVIA AND BENJAMIN WEINSTOCK

The Weinstocks like to keep it casual by dividing the work between the two of them.

For New Yorker and master cake baker Sylvia Weinstock, today's entertaining innovations mean freedom from what she calls "culinary competition." Although Sylvia counts New York's most prestigious restaurateurs and chefs among guests in her Manhattan loft, she feels no pressure to serve "one-upmanship food." Instead, she believes in creating an informal atmosphere that encourages people to "hang out loose" and linger at the table.

Favoring informal dinners, Sylvia always extends her invitations over the telephone. Her one "guest-list tip" for the novice host: "Don't just invite the people you know. Invite the people you want to know." She never uses place cards and keeps her menus simple. Hosting duties are shared with her husband, Benjamin, who does the shopping (according to her carefully constructed list), oversees the bar, and carves when the menu calls for it. Their small dinners are collections of old friends, repeat visitors, and those meeting for the first time. "I invite a group I've thought about—people who will blend or whose interests complement each other," Sylvia says. But that's the only common denominator. "The best part of New York is the diversity. I can put together a group of people with different ages, backgrounds, and occupations, and there will still be some conversational thread. It's very stimulating."

Sylvia likes to gather six to ten people around her large oval table, where guests can "relax and be comfortable—even with their conversation." Because she loves the look of bare wood, she had her walnut table treated with a veneer and simply marks each place with a woven mat. She combines her sterling silver and "good crystal" with Italian and Portuguese ceramics and may even add Mexican glassware. "I love an interesting table," she remarks, "and I love color." An extensive collection of dinnerware enables the hostess to vary her table settings: One dinner may feature a patterned plate for each course; another, plates in the same pattern but in different shades. Flowers are never the focus. When she has flowers at all, Sylvia removes them at dinner, preferring to serve the food family style in decorative bowls and platters so that the meal itself becomes the centerpiece.

Sylvia keeps the atmosphere informal by doing the cooking herself while Benjamin tends bar. The meal starts with "a nibble or two," like cheese or smoked salmon, followed by something homey and uncomplicated. In the winter, this is apt to be a hearty dish that can cook slowly (like osso buco) while she tends to other things, and in the summer something that can be grilled at the last minute (fish or steak). Either way she's free to enjoy the evening along with her guests. Although Sylvia is famous for her decorative wedding cakes, her favorite at-home desserts are poached pears, baked apples, and fruit and cheese. "The reason I don't serve elaborately decorated cakes at home is the same reason why they say shoemaker's children always have holes in their soles," she says philosophically.

After an evening of simple food and good conversation, the Weinstocks often have to remind guests that it's time to go home. "At about eleven o'clock I tell them 'tomorrow's another workday,'" says the hostess. Then I turn to my husband and say 'What a great evening.' And that's why I love to entertain."

The Setting

W E'RE ALL FAMILIAR with those Hollywood images that link sophistication (or the lack thereof) to silverware: the beautiful Natalie Wood reapplying lipstick while using the blade of her dinner knife as a mirror; or Julia Roberts as the poor but "pretty woman," surreptitiously counting the tines of her fork before she feels confident enough to eat her salad. But the best flatware moment on film comes in James Cameron's 1997 box-office hit *Titanic*, when young freight-class traveler Jack Dawson confronts the array of silverware set before him in the first-class dining room and asks, "Are all these for me?" His dinner partner, the unsinkable Molly Brown, offers excellent on- or off-screen advice: "Start at the outside and work your way in."

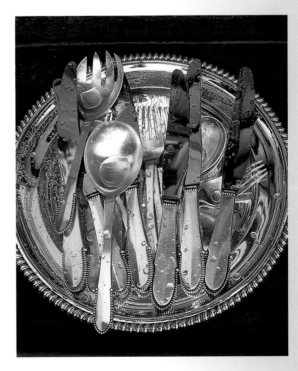

It's really that simple. Think of a place setting as a fully extended accordion that you're about to compress, course by course. Whatever the degree of formality, the variety of the utensils, or the apparent awkwardness of the configuration, silverware is always placed alongside the plate in the order it should be used; forks on the left, knives and spoons on the right. At informal (and some semiformal) meals, dessert utensils rest on the table horizontally, above the dinner plate.

At formal meals, the dessert silverware is presented as needed, along with the dessert course. Tradition also dictates that a place setting never be left empty—one reason why service plates (also called show plates or chargers), are used at some semiformal and all formal dinners. Primarily decorative, these flat, over-sized plates are laid in the center of each place setting in advance of the guests' arrival at table and are cleared only when they can be replaced immediately with the next course. (They can also be left on the table to act as an additional under-plate for the first course.)

The Lap of Luxury

- Napkins have their own rules. They should always be in soft folds, never starched or pressed into shape.
- Standard napkins vary in size from sixteen-inch square, used for more casual dining, to the truly formal version, which can be as large as two feet square. (Regardless of the napkin's size, a guest should unfold it gently, without snapping it open or flapping it around. Larger napkins can be placed on the lap unfolded halfway.)
- Since a napkin is the first thing a guest uses, it should never be placed under the silverware. Napkins are often positioned on the service plate. At an informal dinner, when no such plate is used, they go in the center of the empty setting or to the left of the forks.
- Guests should put their napkins in their laps when they sit down, not when the food is served. (The only exception is a formal dinner, when guests wait and take their cue from the hostess.) A guest leaving the table at any time during the meal should place his or her napkin on the left side of the plate, not on the chair.
- When the hostess places her napkin on the table, it is a signal that dinner is over. Guests should do the same, loosely folding their napkins (any obvious stains on the underside) before placing them on either side, never on top, of the plate.

You can find plenty of how-to books that demonstrate "the art" of elaborate napkin folds, right down to peak and curlicue. But twisting your linens into ornate shapes can give a staged, "Dynasty"-like look to your table. Instead, use a classic fold, and your napkins—vintage or new—will work with any place setting for any occasion.

Square

Start with a rectangle. Fold the napkin over (once or twice depending on the size) to make a square with the right propor-tion for the service plate. Place it on the plate, with the open side to the right.

Cylinder

Start with a rectangle. Fold the napkin lengthwise into thirds and flatten slightly. Place it on the plate, folded side down. (This works best with a larger, dinner-sized napkin.)

Shield

Start with a square. Fold the napkin diagonally to make a triangle, tucking the two side points under. Place the napkin, folded side down, on the plate with the center point toward the guest.

Triangle

Start with a rectangle. Fold the napkin over (once or twice depending on the size) to make a square. Fold the square in half diagonally. Place the triangle next to the forks, with the center point away from the plate. (This works best with smaller, luncheon-size napkins.)

The Night Has a Thousand Eyes

IF YOU FEEL YOU'RE BEING WATCHED, you are. A good serving staff is trained to take their lead from you. Not only are they watching what you eat, they're watching how you eat, waiting for you to send them a silent silverware signal.

I'm not done yet

To position silverware during a pause in the meal, imagine that your plate is the face of a clock. In the continental style, the utensils rest on the rim of your plate (pointing toward each other) in a triangle (open across the bottom), the knife at about eight o'clock, and the fork (tine side down) at about four o'clock. In the American style, the knife and fork (tine side up) rest on the left-hand side of your plate, somewhere between two and five o'clock.

You can take this now

To let your server know that you are finished, place your knife and fork diagonally across the plate with the tips of the utensils resting far enough into the center so that the silverware won't fall off when the plate is removed.

Although they bring their professional expertise to entertaining, George and Jenifer Lang (below) manage to keep their parties feeling personal.

A Family Affair

GEORGE AND JENIFER LANG

FOR GEORGE LANG, the well-known New York restaurateur, and his wife, Jenifer, a culinary authority and manager of the couple's three-star restaurant, Café des Artistes, entertaining at home starts with a brainstorming session. They each write down the names of people they would like to see, then divide their lists into smaller dinner parties of eight to twelve. Invitations go out over the telephone, followed by written reminders. Then the Langs get down to work, making decisions based on their "holy trinity": decoration, cooking, and serving.

"The most complex party can be reduced to the very simple when you start with these three components," says George. The couple uses a basic setup on their large rectangular dining table, starting with a tablecloth (or place mats), followed by service plates on which they place folded napkins. "We like to use a service plate or else the table looks empty when the guests arrive," George says. As for place cards, sometimes they use them, sometimes not. "With a small group, you don't have to be a memo-technician to remember where you want people to sit," George reasons. When place cards are used, they are handwritten in George's distinctive calligraphy on plain heavy stock and positioned atop the napkin. On special occasions, particularly when serving one of their thematic "foodie" dinners, George will also write and illustrate a menu card. The Langs don't go overboard in decorating the table. "Our guests are our decoration," he says. "Sometimes we will have little touches of flowers or a centerpiece of apples. But if someone comments on the arrangement, I feel uneasy. I think it must be overdone."

As one might expect, when it comes to cooking, the Langs do it themselves. Dinner is prepared (mostly by Jenifer) in their professionally equipped kitchen, which is open to the dining room—this culinary couple's equivalent of a home entertainment center. A wide window opening over the counter separating the two rooms makes it possible for plates of food to be casually passed back and forth. On some occasions guests serve themselves from platters set in a dining room hutch lined with built-in warmers.

The couple prefers to have everything ready when people arrive, but on occasion (and especially with close friends), they do complete the meal's final steps together. "We give out jobs—stirring, slicing, completing the table setting—and this can be an amusing part of the evening," George claims. Hors d'oeuvre are rarely served because the Langs believe they take the edge off a guest's appetite for the main meal. But the couple does make Parmesan crackers to accompany the red and white wine, champagne, and sparkling water they offer before dinner. George goes out of his way to get wines he knows their

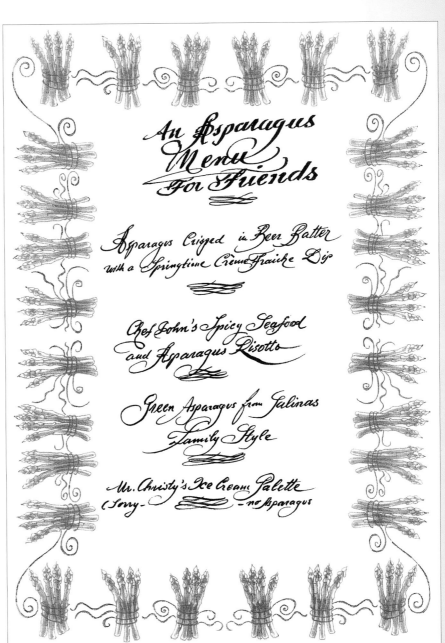

An Asparagus Menu For Friends

Asparagus Crisped in Beer Batter
with a Springtime Crème Fraiche Dip

Chef John's Spicy Seafood
and Asparagus Risotto

Green Asparagus from Salinas
Family Style

Mr. Christy's Ice Cream Palette
(Sorry— — no Asparagus)

Invitations and menu cards are handwritten in George's distinctive style.

guests like, hard-to-find favorites that will come as a surprise. "But no matter how special, we don't continue with the same wines during dinner. The selections change with the food." Occasionally the Langs will have a pitcher of "something fun" for the cocktail hour. "Martinis, of course," George says. But he also likes to make a theme drink, like the *caipirinha*, a Brazilian cocktail made of cachaça, fresh limes, and sugar.

The Langs are constantly experimenting with food and wines they think will please their friends, and menus are often shaped to the particular preferences of a guest of honor. On one occasion this meant serving a friend who loves soup an all-soup dinner, beginning with lobster bisque and continuing with pot-au-feu, the French dish of meat and vegetables in a rich broth. Dessert was zuppa inglese (an Italian dish that resembles trifle, and can be translated as "English soup"). "And way before the architectural concept of deconstruction was part of culinary jargon, we served savory pie shells that had to be reconstructed by the guests, choosing from a selection of fillings like shrimp, chicken, beef ragout, vegetable paella, meatballs, crisp bits of bacon, snipped fresh herbs, and grated cheese."

Whether they are entertaining in their home or at their restaurant, the Langs say that being good hosts comes down to simply giving their guests a few hours of pleasure. And what can a couple who must balance work and family with a reputation for great hospitality do when guests don't want to leave? "We raise our glasses at the end of the evening and say, 'Dear guests, the Lang household rule is that you come at seven. But you leave at eleven.'"

42

Guests, Menu, Action
SERVICE STYLES

OPPOSITE
Just as menus change season to season, different occasions call for different serving techniques.

You've got a room full of guests and a kitchen full of food, and this time the twain must meet. Many factors must be considered before you determine what works for a given occasion, but there are three basic styles of service for a seated party. Although the meal can be served through a combination of these styles (with the main course served by butlers and all other courses arranged on plates in the kitchen), when staff is being used, service should remain unhurried and unobtrusive, almost fading into the background. Generally speaking, service begins with the woman seated to the right of the host, and continues counterclockwise around the table. The host is served last. The hostess begins to eat when she is served, encouraging

others to do the same. All food is served from the left. Beverages are served from the right.

Family style (also called English style):
The food is arranged in serving bowls and platters, placed on the table, and passed from guest to guest. Seconds are served the same way. This informal service style creates lively activity at the table that encourages camaraderie, but it can also interrupt more serious conversation.

Plated (also called American style):
The food is arranged in moderately sized portions on individual plates in the kitchen by the staff. Seconds can be served the same way (the offer is made by the hostess and the plates are refilled in the kitchen) or from a prearranged platter passed from guest to guest.

Butlered:
The food is arranged on serving platters or trays and offered by waiters. The

waiter may present the platter to each guest so that he or she can serve himself (known as Russian style), or the waiter does the serving, transferring the food from the platter to each guest's plate (called French style, and considered to be the most formal service). In either case, the serving tray is held level and lowered to the guest's plate, making service easier and preventing splatters and spills. Seconds are offered in the same manner, except at multicourse formal dinners, when seconds are never served.

Entertaining at a Restaurant

WELL-KNOWN CAFÉ SOCIETY restaurateurs-to-the-stars like David Chasen (Chasen's), "Prince" Michael Romanoff (Romanoff's) of Los Angeles, and Gene Cavallero (The Colony) in New York all had something in common: an uncanny ability to attract celebrities by coddling the big shots. You may not regularly command the choicest table in the room (as Truman Capote did at The Colony) or sit in a booth marked by a bronze plaque bearing your name (like Humphrey Bogart at Romanoff's), but you can still make a restaurant seem like your own private club for the evening.

Whatever the reason, if you decide to host a seated dinner in a restaurant instead of in your home (the number of guests exceed those you can seat comfortably, or it's just plain convenient), attention to detail is key. Select a restaurant with broad appeal (to please all your guests); or, if there is a guest of honor, choose a location with his or her preference in mind. Your invitation should clearly state the name of the restaurant so that people have an idea of how to dress. Include the address and telephone number of the restaurant, in addition to your own telephone number for a response request. If there is a comfortable bar or area designated for cocktails, two-time your invitations (for example, seven-thirty for drinks and dinner at eight). Since it is often difficult to stand and mingle in a crowded restaurant, this is a practical way to assemble your guests and give everyone the chance to get acquainted. Move to your table(s) at the appointed time, leaving word for any late guests to join your party.

Stephen Brown, a New York restaurateur and maître d' with more than twenty years of experience in arranging private parties, offers other valuable tips guaranteed to make any event run smoothly:

- Don't leave anything to chance. If you haven't been to the restaurant before, have a meal there before you make any decisions. Consider the service and the atmosphere as well as the food.

Bigger restaurants have banquet managers; these are the people who should be able to help with every aspect of the party. But no matter who you deal with, make an appointment to meet in the restaurant in order to do the initial planning.

Be very specific about what you want, right down to the shape of the tables (round, square, or long) and in what area you want to be seated. Some restaurants have a party space, and while these rooms may be away from traffic and congestion, they can also seem isolated, lacking the flavor of the restaurant. Ask the banquet manager to let you see where your party will be seated and how the tables will be configured.

By all means, personalize your tables with place cards, flowers, and gifts. But you must collaborate with the banquet manager. Restaurant tables are often smaller than your own dining room table and may not accommodate certain flower arrangements and/or gifts. When you leave goodie bags on the seats, where do your guests put them after they sit down?

Even though you want to arrive early to make sure everything is on track, never greet your guests at the door. This is the job of the maître d'.

The party host and banquet manager may arrange an abbreviated menu of three choices for appetizers, entrées, and desserts at smaller parties. For larger groups, a preselected menu usually works better.

Remember, kitchen time is extremely important in a restaurant; while you can wait fifteen minutes for a late guest, waiting any longer than that before ordering is inexcusable.

The host picks the wine; guests select their own cocktails.

Don't tip a banquet manager; he or she receives a percentage of the cost of the party. However, it helps to tip the maître d' a little something (about $50) before the party starts as a thank-you for getting everything organized (he understands that he can also expect his usual gratuity on the bill).

Make arrangements with the banquet manager for payment so the check does not arrive at the table.

Don't micromanage. Communicate everything ahead of time, confirm on paper and let the restaurant staff do their jobs. Relax. You're returning home to a clean house and a spotless kitchen.

OPPOSITE
Be clear about details during the planning so you can rely on the restaurant staff to create the party you want.

CHAPTER *2*

The Buffet

WE'VE ALL SEEN those fantasy buffets in movies and magazines: the camera capturing rapturous guests with their forks eagerly poised over glistening turkeys and hams, huge bowls of perfectly cooked shrimp, pyramids of fruit and cheese. But what makes a buffet a buffet isn't necessarily an extravaganza of food, and, since many buffets are staffed, it isn't even true that guests always help themselves. A buffet is simply a style of entertaining in which the food being served at the party is arranged on platters and set out on a table, sideboard, or kitchen island. Many hosts decide on buffet service when their guest lists exceed the number they can seat at their dining room tables. However, choosing to entertain buffet style not only determines how the meal is presented, it also dictates what kind of food will be served and how it will be eaten, right down to the silverware needed.

Entertaining in the buffet style is versatile enough to accommodate any crowd—even when your dining table can't. Whether guests are being served one dish or choosing from a variety, find a place to perch or stand and socialize; conversation is always the main course.

The Buffet: Three Ways

Standing

A STANDING BUFFET (also called lap service) is the most casual style. Guests find their silverware (frequently wrapped in napkins) and plates stacked alongside the food. Since the dining room is often where food is served, guests migrate into other rooms. Some are perfectly happy to stand and eat with ease; others make themselves comfortable on couches or perch on stairs, relying on their laps or a flat surface nearby as a place to set down plates. Although it may seem awkward, a standing buffet offers guests the ultimate luxury at a party: the freedom to choose their own dinner companions and change them at will. The menu usually calls for dishes that require a fork only, and dessert is often an assortment of sweets passed on trays, accompanied by cocktail napkins.

A buffet table can be the right place for an extravagant arrangement, as long as it is placed safely out of the way.

Partially Seated

A partially seated buffet means that in addition to the make-do seating your home already offers, small tables are scattered throughout the party space. Rental companies stock thirty-six-inch round tables, or bistro tables, for this purpose (see Chapter Five, page 158). The general rule is to provide seating for about a third of the guests—once you seat more than that (without accommodating every guest), it can look as if you unintentionally left some people without a place to sit. Tables at a partially seated buffet are not preset and typically have no decorations. Once again, the menu is planned around fork-only food, and silverware and plates are stacked on the buffet table. Dessert may be served buffet-style or put on plates in the kitchen and passed.

Fully Seated

The fully seated buffet is the most formal style, in which you provide a seat for every guest and preset tables right down to decorations and place cards, just as you would for a seated dinner. As in all other types of buffet, guests go to the buffet table for their main course. Additional courses, like salad and dessert, are plated in the kitchen and served by the staff. Because every guest has a place to sit, and the appropriate silverware can be included in the table settings, the menu is not limited to fork-only food.

The best buffet arrangement keeps the food accessible and easy to manage.

53

Form and Function

WHEN IT COMES TO POSITIONING THE BUFFET, you might think you're creating more room by pushing your table against a wall. But unless your party is small enough to be accommodated by sideboard service, a buffet table with access from only one side is like a dam impeding the free flow of guests and causing a traffic backup. Not only is there less congestion when your guests can walk completely around the buffet station, but placing food platters on both sides of the table (reserving flowers and candles for the center) creates a

Who's On First?

Etiquette once called upon the oldest woman at the party to start the buffet. But try getting someone to admit to that distinction, even if it means going first. Although it is wise to announce dinner to small groups (in an attempt to avoid the inevitable crush at the buffet), be prepared to walk the first guests to and through the line to get the buffet off and running.

A Buffet Menu

- When planning your menu, remember that a smorgasbord and a buffet are not the same thing. Although the term "smorgasbord" (from the Swedish for "bread-and-butter table") has come to mean an all-you-can-eat buffet featuring a variety of dishes, a buffet can also consist of a single main course with several accompanying side dishes.

- Offering more than one main course (what caterers call a split entrée) is advisable only when your guest list exceeds twenty-five. This is because splitting the main course means reducing the quantities offered. For example, should two main courses be offered, the serving platters would contain half a portion of each dish per person instead of a full portion.

- When the number of guests is small, half-portions can make for a rather meager presentation, defeating the idea of abundance. Instead, choose a main course that you think most guests will enjoy (like a simple grilled chicken or roast meat) and add variety with an assortment of side dishes.

- Select dishes that can survive on the buffet without too much fuss. Avoid anything that requires last-minute preparation, split-second timing, or the need to be served piping hot.

- One-dish meals (like baked pasta or chili) have always been buffet favorites. Grilled meat and chicken (presliced) and seafood salads are also popular, particularly when accompanied by easy-to-eat vegetables (such as asparagus) and rice dishes (more manageable than potatoes if guests are standing).

- Serve dishes that are cooked in a sauce, like a stew or chili, with a slotted serving spoon to drain excess liquid.

- Meats should be precarved. This is a matter of speed and presentation; there is simply no way to keep a partially carved roast looking appealing. Sauces should always be served on the side.

- And if you plan on serving a salad, consider chopped greens, which are neater to serve and eat than leafy lettuces.

double buffet line. Serving from both sides of a buffet station also produces a more sociable atmosphere. Guests are able to chat across the table: a pleasant diversion while they wait in line.

On the Riviera

LYNN AND OSCAR WYATT JR.

Lynn Wyatt and husband Oscar play host safari-style.

LYNN WYATT, A TEXAS HOSTESS considered by many to be the life of her own parties, celebrates her birthday each year with her husband, Oscar Wyatt Jr., at a seated buffet in the garden of their villa in the South of France. The Wyatts' party is so eagerly anticipated that Lynn doesn't even have to send out invitations; people just know to hold that date. But since this party is always planned around a theme, what the guests don't know until they get Lynn's telephone call is where her imagination will be taking them. One year the "destination" was Havana, and each table was named after the city's well-known streets, like Plaza de la Revolution. The thematic menu featured lemon chicken, black beans, and rice with chorizo. There was music to match: a Cuban band entertained during the cocktail hour, a three-piece combo played softly during dinner, and the two groups combined to make a Latin-influenced dance band later in the evening.

Another time the theme was Hollywood, and since Lynn thinks of flash-bulbs popping "à la movie premieres," she gave the guests disposable cameras as they arrived. "When it was time for everyone to get their table cards, Elton John, Joan Collins, and Quincy Jones were snapping pictures like they were 'glamorous paparazzi,'" she says. Another year Lynn "went Safari" and tells how the men came wearing camouflage jackets and pith helmets. Helmet Newton even had a huge fake snake wrapped around his neck. "'Denim and Diamonds' was another fun theme," she continues. "My European guests loved dressing in Western garb, and they looked fabulous." But her gypsy theme was probably the most successful, with colorful fringed tablecloths, fortune tellers, and romantic gypsy-flamenco music. "That party went late into the night," Lynn says.

Set up on a raised terrace, the alfresco buffet table is a dramatic focal point; seven oval tables, each set for ten, are positioned on the lawn below. All take advantage of the huge sweeping view, starting with the port of Beaulieu and extending to Saint-Jean-Cap-Ferrat. Then, on the right, you can see

Lynn's annual birthday buffet has a way of turning from dinner to dancing.

57

Villefranche. "It is magnificent, day or night," says Lynn. "And if the moon hangs in there, well, it is spectacular." Adding to the beauty of the landscape, Lynn uses lots of votive candles on the tables as well as flickering torches set into the lawn. "I think people are more at ease in a resort atmosphere, and that's what I try to create," Lynn says.

Since buffet etiquette can vary from party to party, even the most experienced guests may not be able to anticipate what a host has in mind when it comes time to serve. As a result, it helps to act as a guide, letting guests know what to expect. Lynn seats her guests at their respective tables to visit for a few minutes before calling them to the buffet. The long rectangular buffet table has a double line, so that guests can approach from both sides. "But people don't mind if they have to wait a few minutes. They stand in line chattering away and admiring each other's costumes," Lynn says.

In anticipation of the meal to come, Lynn never serves hors d'oeuvre. "I have an excellent French chef and serve plenty of food," says the hostess. "I don't like my guests to fill up on finger food before sitting down to dinner." Instead, waiters circulate with trays of red and white wine as well as water and a special cocktail that reflects the evening's theme while guests concentrate on conversation and the view.

After everyone has eaten (and some have had seconds), the main course buffet is converted into an extravagant dessert display. Some of the desserts are matched to the party theme (in the case of the Cuban-inspired menu, coconut crème caramel and nougat ice cream), but Lynn always serves a Southern-style fruit salad and pecan pie—because "it is so popular."

Lynn Wyatt's Dinner in a Tropical Paradise

FIRST COURSE
Crab Cakes
Slices of Ham and Papaya
Chicken and Coconut Salad
Ceviche

MAIN COURSE
Brochette of Beef with Pineapple
Tenderloin of Veal with Ginger Sauce
Rice with Almonds
Sweet Potato Gratin Creole
Galette de Mais
(Corn Pancake with Red and Green Peppers)

DESSERT
Banana and Mango Flambé
Lemon Cake with White Chocolate Frosting
Pecan Pie
Coconut Ice Cream with Toasted Coconut Flakes
Fruit Salad

Flights of Fancy

For Lynn Wyatt, a party should be inspired by a theme not dictated by it. Although her guests may dress the part, her parties are not costume parties, Lynn says. "If someone hasn't considered the theme when dressing, I don't want them to feel uncomfortable when they arrive."

This once-a-year party is the only time Lynn likes to entertain at a buffet. Guests always have the chance to come together during cocktail hour (whether a party is seated or not), but serving a buffet gives them the opportunity to continue mingling while they stand in line—a big bonus, since many guests use Lynn's birthday party to catch up on a year's worth of activities.

After dessert, Lynn encourages guests to move from the tables on the lawn to the terrace. "It's like shifting from the dining room to the living room when you're giving a seated party indoors," she says. Coffee and herbal teas are served, and the band begins to play. Some guests will stay and linger at the tables if good conversation is flowing. My greatest compliment is when a guest tells me, 'Our table was the best table this year,'" says Lynn.

To keep it all straight, Lynn keeps an encyclopedic party book, chronicling everything from practical matters, like the number of car valets, to creative considerations, like table decorations. Since she always has a photographer at the party, Lynn also has album after album of pictures, grouped according to years and themes; she leaves the albums out on a table during each party. "Guests love to look at them; they see themselves and their friends from so many years back. It's like experiencing the previous parties all over again," she says.

Does a confident hostess like Lynn Wyatt have a plan for bad weather? She admits to praying, lighting candles, and practicing rain-stay-away dances. "It works. At least it has so far."

In Manhattan

PAMELA FIORI AND COLT GIVNER

PAMELA FIORI, EDITOR-IN-CHIEF OF *TOWN & COUNTRY*, serves a buffet when she and her husband, Colt Givner, are having a dinner party for more than fourteen guests, the maximum number that can comfortably

Pamela Fiori presides over the dessert selection at her holiday buffet.

be seated at their dining room table. "I reserve buffet-style entertaining for those occasions when I want a casual, relaxed feeling, or when I find myself entertaining larger groups, like staff parties and other gatherings around the holidays," she says. But that atmosphere doesn't materialize without care and concern on her part. It takes a lot of work to keep a buffet together, she says. "You have to be on the move constantly, checking on people in different rooms and moving them around when necessary—especially if one special guest is being monopolized unmercifully." The buffet is set out on the couple's dining room table and adjacent sideboard (if more room is needed). "I don't put flowers in either place," Pamela says. "I will do arrangements elsewhere

For Family or Friends

PASSED HORS D'OEUVRE

Gamberi Tonnati

(*Shrimp with Tuna Caper Dip*)

Slow-Roasted Roma Tomato and Gorgonzola

Dolce Crostini

ON THE BUFFET

Sliced Rosemary Lemon Chicken Breasts with

Grilled Radicchio and Endive

Oven-Roasted Asparagus

Orecchiette with Wild Mushrooms

Black Olive Bread Sticks

Rolls

(*Semolina with Fennel, Golden Raisin*)

Passed Sweets

Brownies

(*Chocolate, Cappuccino*)

Lemon Walnut Squares

For the Holidays

PASSED HORS D'OEUVRE

Crab Cakes

Spinach Quesadillas

ON THE BUFFET

Ham with Bourbon and Maple Syrup Glaze

Sweet Grainy Mustard

Apple Chutney and Cranberry Walnut Conserve

Cabbage, Parsley, and Carrot Slaw with

Red Wine and Chile Pepper Vinaigrette

Artisan American Cheeses

Cornbread

Small Sandwich Rolls

Passed Sweets

Decorated Christmas Cookies

(*Sugar, Chocolate, Ginger Spice*)

Clementines

Medjool Dates

in the apartment, but I don't think flowers belong on the buffet table; that's where the food goes. And watch the candles. If there was ever a time for the whole place to go up in flames, it's during a crowded buffet party when people are reaching over the table." The hostess uses a tablecloth and, underneath, a protective mat. "I have no qualms about mixing china and flatware patterns if necessary, and almost always mix the napkin colors. The only requirement is that anything I select contributes to a harmonious table."

Pamela lays out the buffet table by stacking the plates on each end and creating two food lines, starting with the entrées. "I place the silverware last— always wrapped with a napkin into a neat package—on the buffet line so guests don't have to juggle it along with their plates," she explains. Pamela keeps the food simple as well. "My instinct is that all the food you serve buffet style should be room temperature and easily eaten with a fork or your fingers. I'd categorize this kind of food as 'crowd pleasers.' If the food you're serving doesn't do that, why serve it?"

Before dinner, guests are served from a full bar. "I want people to know they can drink whatever their heart desires," says Pamela, although she finds

that most of them stick to wine and sparking water. "I think they do this out of consideration for whomever is tending bar, and in the interest of getting a drink fast and not holding up other people," she explains. Pamela sticks to a basic stemmed wineglass and double old-fashioned glasses (her own for smaller parties; rented for larger gatherings). She never uses precious stemware. "I can remember being at a party where drinks were being passed on trays in long-stemmed crystal vessels, several of which went crashing to the floor. I could tell from the sound—and so could everyone else—that this was the 'good stuff,' and I felt so sorry for the waiter who was serving the drinks—the glasses were heavy and unwieldy."

Hors d'oeuvre are passed, but not too many. "Otherwise my guests fill up fast and don't go the buffet table when they're called, and that makes for a long night," says Pamela.

While some buffet guests stand and eat as a matter of preference, Pamela would rather they sit. "I like to set up a few sitting areas in various parts of the apartment so there will be cozy places where people can gather," she says. Since people will be milling around the buffet table and drifting into other rooms to eat, she suggests clearing away anything that is fragile or extremely valuable. You don't want to put your guests in a position where they might break something you really treasure.

While her dessert buffet is being set up, Pamela ushers guests into the living room and offers some kind of entertainment—often someone at the piano playing standards. This empties out the dining room quickly so that the staff can clear the table and set it up with sweets. Sometimes, if the entertainment goes on for a while and everyone has made themselves comfortable, she asks the staff to put together a few trays of sweets and pass them along with decaffeinated coffee in demitasse cups. When there is a special-occasion cake (for a birthday or anniversary), after the toast, she likes to have that cake put on plates and served in the living room as well. In either case, Pamela warns, "Don't be surprised if your guests stay and stay."

The Buffet Napkin Fold

Because a napkin wrapped around silverware can unwind, the best buffet napkin fold is flat (like a spatula) with a pocket in which to tuck the silverware.

64

1) Start by folding the napkin into a square, positioning the open fold on the left and the "four pages" of fabric in the upper-right-hand corner. **2)** Fold one "page" diagonally to the lower-left-hand corner. **3)** Flip the napkin over (without rotating it). **4)** Make two lengthwise folds by bringing the bottom edge to the middle of the square and folding the top half down to match. **5)** When you flip the napkin over again, you will have a long flat cylinder with a diagonal pocket.

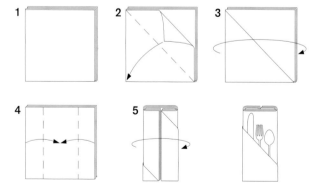

Always stack the napkin bundles on a tray that can be quickly and easily moved if the configuration of the table should change. Stack the napkins as if you're building a log cabin: four bundles horizontally (as the base), four bundles vertically (as the next level) and so on.

Keep Your Buffet Running Smoothly

- If possible, place the buffet table near the kitchen to make replenishing easier and faster.

- When it comes to arranging food, your foremost goal should be to minimize accidents, minor to major. Unless you live on a cruise ship, there is no need for food platters perched atop decorative stands and overturned baskets spilling out a jumble of bread and rolls. Keep your table design simple and the food accessible by picking flat-bottomed platters and bowls that won't tip.

- The best serving utensils require only one hand to use, like salad tongs. Instead of serving forks and spoons, pastry or asparagus tongs can also be used to serve sliced meats. Allow enough space next to each serving platter for a small plate so guests have a place to rest the serving utensils.

- Rather than large serving dishes, smaller dishes (with back-ups ready in the kitchen for easy replenishing) keep a buffet looking fresh and appealing, no matter how many people have already been served.

- Plan your menu to avoid chafing dishes. Not only do they make any buffet (no matter how elegant) resemble a cafeteria line, but the heat source can't be regulated and food continues to cook. If you do decide to serve a hot dish (like a stew or chili), small serving dishes and frequent replenishing will keep the food hot enough.

- Even when you are offering fork-only food, have knives available upon request. But don't put them on the buffet table unless you have one for everyone.

- Before the party, outline a table plan by arranging serving dishes and trays on the buffet station until you determine the perfect arrangement. Write the name of each menu item (along with a description of its proper serving utensil) on a Post-it and stick it in the appropriate empty serving piece so the staff can re-create the table design.

- Beverages should not be placed on the food table; the guests have enough to handle. Let people settle wherever they are sitting (or standing) and then have the staff circulate with trays holding glasses of prepoured wine and water. The trays can also be set up on a conveniently placed table or sideboard.

- Despite all the careful planning to make your buffet run smoothly and quickly, there will always be a few guests who hold up the line by staring at the selections, as though deciding how many spears of asparagus to put on their plates is the most important decision they'll ever make. There is no way a host can rush a guest through a buffet table without sounding like a traffic cop; rely on a staff member to step in and offer help.

- At buffets, "seconds" are offered in two ways: Guests can return to the buffet station and refill their own plates, or staff members can circulate, offering to pass through the buffet line on the guest's behalf. Either way, you will need more plates, silverware, and napkins than you have people.

The Sociable Kitchen

JAMES AND JENNIFER D'AURIA

IN 1974, when architect James D'Auria went out on his own, he had two commissions, and both of them were for kitchens. Even now, with a business that has since extended into entire homes, the kitchen remains his favorite room—and none more so than his own.

The D'Aurias' home, in the Hamptons hamlet of Amagansett, New York (once a weekend house and now the couple's permanent residence), has a large square kitchen (twenty-five by twenty-five feet): an open, airy space with room enough to cook and entertain simultaneously. James designed the kitchen to function around several basic activities: a dining area; the food-prep part (oven, sink, and dishwasher); the island (not only for separating workspace from traffic flow but a great place "for conversations"); and the fireplace (which creates

OVERLEAF
Entertaining in an eat-in kitchen gives your guests a front-row seat.

Working together in full view of their guests, James and Jennifer D'Auria have nothing to hide and no place to hide it.

another sitting area). As beautiful as the kitchen is, it is not just a showplace. James and his wife, Jennifer, an actress and real estate agent, entertain frequently. The couple, who fittingly met at a dinner party, like company in their kitchen. (After all, they reason, the kitchen is where people tend to gather anyway.) They also don't mind help and welcome anyone who wants to bring a dish or contribute the wines—after a discussion with the cooks about their menu, of course.

Your kitchen may not be as conveniently outfitted as the D'Aurias', but it can be as sociable. Although a meal served from the kitchen is less ceremonial, there are still some guidelines to keep the evening relaxed, for the cooks as well as the guests:

> ❧ Whether your kitchen is open to the rest of the house or adjoins the dining area, the "real cooking" (the chopping and stirring and whisking) should be done in advance. No matter how inviting a kitchen supper can seem, no one really wants to see you cook. A room temperature-menu or one dish (like a casserole or stew) warming on the stove in a tidy kitchen when the guests arrive is ideal.

> ❧ Get and stay organize by clearing counters and making sure all the cooking utensils are washed and out of sight by the time the doorbell rings.

> ❧ Separate food from bar offerings to help keep traffic flowing. Use soft, recessed lighting or under-the-counter lighting to highlight each area.

CHAPTER 3
Cocktail Parties and the Open House

APPLE MARTINI

CHOCOLATE MARTINI

CLASSIC MARTINI

COSMOPOLITAN

AS ENTERTAINING STYLES, the cocktail party and open house may go in and out of vogue, but their trademark eclectic guest mix and come-all camaraderie remain prime examples of American ingenuity—social innovations that can be traced back to the Roaring Twenties when prohibition went into full effect. Although Herbert Hoover's "noble experiment" put the padlock on corner saloons, it inadvertently produced an underground of basement dives and makeshift nightclubs selling bootleg whiskey in coffee cups. Revelers merely whispered a password through a slot in a locked door to gain admittance, and by the middle of the decade there were an estimated 32,000 "speakeasies" in New York City, including the famed Twenty-one Club and The Stork Club. Despite occasional raids, the police couldn't enforce prohibition, and drinkers shared a boisterous esprit de corps that came along with flouting the law. There was an air of reckless gaiety in the illicit "gin joints" of the Jazz Age.

The right people in the right place for just the right amount of time is the mix and mingle formula for the perfect cocktail party.

Prohibition sparked a cultural revolution that cut across social barriers, making kindred spirits out of bootlegging gangsters and otherwise law-abiding citizens.

"Hello, suckers" was celebrated hostess Texas Guinan's trademark greeting to patrons at her infamous Manhattan club, El Fay, and for the first time in nightlife history, the word "suckers" was applied to both men and women. Having entered the workforce during World War I, many women chose not to return to their previous sheltered existence, transforming themselves into the era's "bachelor girls": bobbing their hair, shortening their skirts, and smoking and drinking in public. Since hard liquor was easier to manufacture than beer or wine, speakeasy owners, eager to encourage the sale of distilled spirits, added sugary mixers and fruit juices to their harsh bootleg liquor—and the cocktail was born.

By the time prohibition was repealed in 1933, the cocktail party was a noisy, smoky institution. Hollywood gave the world a romanticized view, portraying the cocktail party as an ultrachic style of entertaining. Movie hosts ranged from the incomparable cocktail couple, William Powell and Myrna Loy (as the witty,

Nick and Nora Charles (Myrna Loy and William Powell) remain film's first couple of the cocktail party.

In *Breakfast at Tiffany's*, Audrey Hepburn set the standard for cocktail party style.

urbane Nick and Nora Charles in the 1930s film series *The Thin Man*), to Rosalind Russell's unforgettable madcap hostess who served pickled rattlesnake canapés and flaming cocktails in the 1958 film adaptation of the Patrick Dennis novel *Auntie Mame*. "There now," she said, holding up a fiery glass to her bewildered guests. "Are we all lit?"

But the true heyday of the cocktail party came after World War II, during the Eisenhower fifties and early sixties. Audrey Hepburn's waifish character Holly Golightly may have enjoyed *Breakfast at Tiffany's* (the 1961 film classic), but she spent almost every night having cocktails, elegantly attired in the little black sheath that has become part of fashion history. Never had the cocktail party seemed more like a gateway into a glamorous evening. All that changed during the late sixties as a rebellious Woodstock Nation warned the world not to trust anyone over thirty, and a single on-screen moment captured the cocktail party's fall from grace. In the 1967 film *The Graduate*, Ben Braddock (played by Dustin

Hoffman) is cornered at his parents' party by a guest who whispers, "I just want to say one word to you—just one word. 'Plastics.'" With that "one word," cocktail parties (and the people who went to them) came to represent everything that was middle class and middle aged: The Establishment.

Even if you were invited to a cocktail party during the next two decades, there were probably two things missing: cocktails and canapés. As aerobic classes replaced happy hour in the 1970s and 1980s, self-restrained Spartans sipped white wine spritzers while they munched carrot sticks and waved away any trace of cigarette smoke, stifling the life of the cocktail party. However, trend-spotters were soon heralding a new "cocktail nation," and the 1996 film *Swingers* glorified the life of lounge lizards, complete with oversized martinis, big band music, and swing dancing. Although the imperative "Get a nightlife" was bannered across that film poster, history has shown that it takes more than top-shelf liquor and retromusic to make a successful cocktail party. It takes a room full of engaging people and a worldly host who knows how to keep his guests well-stirred, never shaken.

The Art of the Cocktail Party

LEE MINDEL

For Lee Mindel, whose loft boasts wide-screen views of the Manhattan skyline that add to the glamour of any evening, hosting a cocktail party meets every entertaining need. Although Lee, a partner with Peter Shelton in the award-winning New York architectural firm Shelton, Mindel & Associates, is recognized for his ability to integrate interiors, architecture, and landscape into a seamless environment for clients, he confesses to being the kind of guy who keeps his shirts in the oven. With an all-consuming work load, he cannot always make the time to attend dinner parties, and never gives them. Lee prefers cocktail parties, confident and at ease with the belief that he doesn't have to be Julia Child in the kitchen, or a premier party organizer like Perle Mesta, yet he can stage a special, creative event.

When Betty Comden and the late Adolph Green's 1949 musical *On the Town* was enjoying a revival on Broadway, Lee was inspired to host an elegant, old-fashioned cocktail party for the lyric and libretto–writing team whose film and stage work have helped mold the world's view of New York, New York as a "helluva town." By choosing a Monday night for the party (when theaters are "dark") and planning with the kind of care usually reserved for seated parties, Lee was able to put together a show-stopping guest list of actors, writers, and producers that was more of an extended family reunion than cocktail party.

"I knew I wanted to give a large party and still create an atmosphere of intimacy that would support everything Betty and Adolph stand for: their warmth and sense of humor," says the host. Since the party was in their honor, Lee started planning the guest list by asking Comden and Green for their choices; then he added his own close friends and others he knew who would love to help celebrate. Even though a hundred people accepted his invitation, Lee's thoughtful planning ensured that there was a thread of common interest running through the party.

Although Lee normally issues cocktail party invitations two to three weeks before the gathering, the Comden-Green invitation, designed by Lee and his staff and custom-printed, was mailed out with a month's notice. "I always assume that many people won't RSVP at all (or wait until the last moment) but still show up. In this case, though, I called around with reminders to people who hadn't responded, especially those I knew the guests of honor would be happy to see."

When he throws a party to honor someone's accomplishments, Lee believes it is important for the host to show respect, in a creative way, for the people being celebrated, and for him, this transcends everything else—the food, the flowers, the bar. To pay tribute to Comden and Green, he put together a party tape of their music, with many of the same songs interpreted by different artists. To further commemorate the event, each guest received a copy of the musical compilation tape, and Lee kept his own record: an *On the Town* guest book bearing the signatures of all the partygoers, starting with the guests of honor.

When it comes to preparing his home, Lee likes to connect the "look" to the occasion. That wasn't so difficult for the Comden and Green party: He just used the incomparable skyline outside his windows as a backdrop. "I was lucky," says Lee. "For that party, I could provide the ultimate set. We lit the water tower on the rooftop terrace, and it felt like a production of

Lee Mindel delivers an extra special celebratory touch: a musical theme cake.

75

Lee Mindel's Party Mix

You may not be entertaining the legendary lyricists themselves, but Comden and Green can still make their presence known at your party. You could hardly ask for a more sophisticated soundtrack.

- "Just in Time" (*Bells Are Ringing*)
- "Comes Once in a Lifetime" (*Subways Are for Sleeping*)
- "Lucky to Be Me" (*On the Town*)
- "Ohio" (*Wonderful Town*)
- "Some Other Time" (*On the Town*)
- "It's Love" (*Wonderful Town*)
- "Make Someone Happy" (*Do, Re, Mi*)
- "New York, New York (a helluva town)" (*On the Town*)
- "The Party's Over" (*Bells Are Ringing*)

Lee prefers hors d'oeuvre
with minimal decoration and
maximum flavor.

West Side Story." The building's water tower typically plays a part in his party planning, and Lee uses it with a "if you can't hide it, let it join the party" practicality—once he strung banks and banks of white lights for a Christmas cocktail party, including a "sort-of-cheesy Santa" hanging off the ladder in midair. While planning a retirement party for Lou Gropp (the former editor-in-chief of *House Beautiful*), Lee called Gropp's wife to ask about some of his favorite things. "! found out that he loves the color orange, so I covered the water tower ladder with orange construction net. Actually, it's still up there."

Inside the loft, instead of flowers, Lee prefers to use green leafy things (like lady's mantle and banana leaves) that relate to the rooftop garden, integrating the two spaces. In the smaller and more isolated parts of the loft, he might use flowers—but just bunches, no "arrangements." "I just use them to add to the sense that something special is happening," says Lee, who takes care of the greens and flowers himself because he doesn't want them to look "done." "Once something looks 'arranged,' the whole party tips over into having the appearance of a stuffy catered affair." He also likes to make things look festive with light—diffused and focused lamplight, as well as votive candles.

Lee also has a few requirements for the food. Working with a caterer, he selects "recognizable food," concentrating on the quality of the ingredients rather than a fussy presentation. He likes simple hors d'oeuvre, like pigs in blankets, or what he considers "clean canapés"—food that is easy to eat and not too elaborate or messy. "I think food that requires too much coordination to pick up, hold, or carry is dangerous," he says. Rotating an assortment of platters and trays varies the look of the food, he adds, so that people don't feel they're getting the same thing every time.

Although Lee is convinced that everyone understands that the word "cocktails" on an invitation is a euphemism for "not dinner," he likes to have enough food (or a simple dish ready in the refrigerator) so that if a few people linger, he has something to offer them. "It's important to remember that cocktail parties have a way of running long—but that makes them even more fun," says Lee.

Large parties at Lee's two-story loft call for two bars: one outside on the roof and one at the foot of the stairs inside. Standard-sized rental tables, covered with his own Belgian linen to add a personal look, are stocked with all-purpose glasses. Considering his museum-quality furnishings and light color scheme, one can't blame Lee for admitting that colored juices and red wine indoors make him a little nervous. No one misses them. The bar is simple but satisfying: basic spirits, wine and champagne, with one or two cocktails of choice, like martinis and Manhattans, as well as nonalcoholic beverages. Lee varies the bar offerings with the weather. "I've got to tell you, in the summer nothing is better than Gatorade and vodka," he says.

For all of his attention to detail, Lee is a relaxed host who likes his parties to feel spontaneous and exciting. "There are a certain freedom and fantasy that come along with a cocktail party invitation," he says. "There are no commitment issues. You can connect with someone and still move around. You may even meet someone, and before you know it, a cocktail party turns into dinner."

What's Your Hurry?

When your party winds down to a few good friends, it's nice to have a quick-fix meal on hand. After an evening of hors d'oeuvre, a simple robust one-dish meal (paired with crusty bread and a green salad) will prove irresistible, even to the most sophisticated palate. In cold weather, favorites like chili, beef stew, lasagna, or an old-fashioned macaroni and cheese casserole get a warm welcome. In the summer, sesame noodles tossed with shrimp or chicken and a cold tomato salad are anyone's idea of a perfect nightcap.

79

How to Decode a Cocktail Party Invitation

"Come for drinks"

This is the least formal kind of cocktail gathering. Invitations are typically extended over the telephone, with little advance notice, to a handful of guests.

- The party often precedes an event that the guests and the host(s) will be attending together, like a concert, the ballet, or even dinner in a restaurant.
- The party is rarely catered, although household staff may serve.
- Drinks vary from wine and champagne to offerings from a full bar, including nonalcoholic beverages.
- Food is simple and casually presented: bowls of nibbles like nuts, olives, and cheese crackers rather than passed hors d'oeuvre. On special occasions, there may be something more substantial, like caviar or smoked salmon, but nothing that constitutes a meal.

"Cocktails and hors d'oeuvre"

Invitations (either custom-printed or fill-in-the-blanks) are issued through the mail, always carry a time limit (like six-thirty to eight-thirty), and more often than not a response request.

- The party is catered and staffed.
- Drinks include wine (and/or champagne), spirits, and specialty cocktails, like martinis or Manhattans.
- The food, generally passed hors d'oeuvre, with bowls of nibbles (olives and nuts) placed casually through the party space, is not intended as dinner.

"Cocktail supper" (or "cocktail buffet")

Invitations, typically issued through the mail, may or may not set time limits.

- The party is often catered and staffed.
- Drinks usually include wine and offerings from a limited spirits bar that may or may not include specialty cocktails.
- No-knife foods, served buffet style (often with small plates and forks), may also include several passed hors d'oeuvre, and are substantial enough to be considered dinner.

The Fashionable Cocktail Party

ADRIENNE AND GIANLUIGI VITTADINI

ADRIENNE VITTADINI'S GRACIOUS APPROACH to entertaining goes a long way toward restoring the glamour of the social cocktail party. Adrienne and her husband, Gianluigi, host two cocktail gatherings a year: a Christmas party in town and a summer event in the country. "I don't always have the time to spend at small dinner parties," says the fashion and home decor designer. "Cocktail parties are my chance to see friends and give them the opportunity to meet each other." Although she starts with a list of close friends, Adrienne is not afraid to mix people, and finds it boring when everyone has the same background. Her guest lists range from bankers to those in the arts, Europeans and Americans. "My goal is for the party to have personality," Adrienne says.

Custom-printed invitations are sent through the mail with at least three weeks' notice. Although the invitations always include a response request, Adrienne also telephones guests the week before the party if she has not heard from them. According to the designer, putting a dress code on an invitation is not really an issue anymore, unless you are specifying black-tie. She trusts that most of her guests automatically know how to dress, or they will call and ask. When they are going to a party directly from work, Adrienne thinks most women plan their wardrobes accordingly. "If women prefer chic dark colors, they may carry a shawl with them, or a little pick-me-up-and-sparkle accessory," she explains.

One of the couple's party priorities is greeting guests. Adrienne and her husband alternate staying close to the door, and both make a big effort to introduce guests to each other. "I think it keeps the party flowing," she says. Adrienne also tries to keep things light and happy with the right music. For summer

In town or the country, Adrienne and Gianluigi Vittadini use the cocktail party as a way to catch up with friends.

parties in the Hamptons, live music adds a "nice little twist." And at Christmas in the city, she hires carolers to help greet the guests because the singers make such an immediate impact and add drama. "For the rest of the evening I use the kind of music I would use at fashion shows: something soft and jazzy, or French and Italian music. But I am very careful with the volume because the noise level at cocktail parties is already high."

Essential to the planning is a well-stocked bar: white wine and champagne, with cocktails (like gin and tonic or martinis) on request. Although Adrienne admits (like most hosts) to being careful about serving beverages that stain when spilled, in the summer she still adds something seasonal, like a rosy-hued Campari and soda. Service also varies with the season. In the city, the couple have a small separate pantry with a bar where the staff prepare drinks. The butlers take orders from the guests as well as circulate with trays of prepoured drinks. In the country, the hosts like to set up a bar near the pool, but also have butlers circulating with trays. "It can be so difficult to get near the bar, and I think it is always nice when your drink is brought to you," Adrienne says.

Adrienne pays special attention to planning the menu, concentrating on passed one-bite hors d'oeuvre because she feels these work best for the guests. "I don't think people can move comfortably with a little plate in their hand, and it can be terribly hard to balance food and a drink."

Classic Canapés and Hors d'Oeuvre

THERE'S A REASON WHY James Beard is often referred to as the "father of the modern hors d'oeuvre." As proprietor of a food store and catering company, Hors d'Oeuvre, Inc. (opened in New York City in 1937), Beard, who looked upon the cocktail party as a "twentieth-century salon," was an entertaining pioneer. His landmark book *Hors D'Oeuvres & Canapés* (1940) was the first devoted exclusively to cocktail party food. In it, Beard makes the fine distinction between canapés and hors d'oeuvre. Canapés (which he refers to as "doots") are "savory butters and pastes on a bed of toast or biscuit or pastry shell," while hors d'oeuvre are "small, tasty bites, usually without bread or biscuit, sometimes on a toothpick and sometimes under their own power."

When you are planning an hors d'oeuvre menu, there's no need for trendy ingredients and exotic combinations. Beard's robust American appetite and love of full-flavored food created hors d'oeuvre that are still being served, despite changing styles.

The James Beard Hors d'Oeuvre Hall of Fame
- Steak tartare balls
- Parma ham rolls
- Artichoke hearts stuffed with pâté

- 🍃 Curried cheese balls
- 🍃 Chunks of cold lobster in cucumber cups
- 🍃 Tiny tomatoes stuffed with chicken salad
- 🍃 Scallop bouchées (lightly creamed scallops in a tiny patty shell)
- 🍃 Bacon tartlets
- 🍃 Cheese puffs
- 🍃 Chicken and mushroom croquettes

As the cocktail languished during the last several decades of entertaining, cocktail party food suffered as well. The formality of small, carefully made hors d'oeuvre gave way to an "anything goes" food philosophy as caterers began serving what they loosely termed "finger food." These included everything from oversized wedges of frittata to tiny (but messy) lamb chops (bone and all). But just because you can eat something with your fingers doesn't mean you should, and the best hors d'oeuvre remain those that can make the trip cleanly and safely from the serving tray to your mouth in one bite.

Canapés and
Hors d'Oeuvre Wisdom

JEAN PRICE

A MEMPHIS HOSTESS who thinks she may have given "too many cocktail parties" over the years, Jean Price has distinct criteria when it comes to hors d'oeuvre. "Small, small, small" is her entertaining mantra. Guests should be able to take an hors d'oeuvre off the tray and put it in their mouths in one bite. When food takes two bites, the first goes in your mouth, the other goes down the front of what you're wearing or on the rug—and Jean has seen lots of these mishaps occur. "I know people think they're doing something wonderful by serving you one of those extra-large shrimp. But the last thing you should have to do at a cocktail party is watch someone struggle to bite an hors d'oeuvre in half," she explains.

**"Keep it simple," advises
Jean Price. "And keep it neat."**

Experience has also taught Jean that hors d'oeuvre should be offered to the guests ready-to-eat. "I once served this wonderful chicken pâté by arranging it on a beautiful platter and surrounding it with melba toast; no one touched it. I took it into the kitchen, cut it into tiny pieces and passed it on the melba toast as a one-bite hors d'oeuvre and it vanished," she says. "Elaborate displays of food may be a good idea on paper; they just don't work at cocktail parties."

Jean believes in giving people what they like: artichoke bottoms with cream cheese and caviar, stuffed mushrooms with bacon and Parmesan, little warm turnovers with wild mushrooms and ground meat. "I don't want people to go home and have a bowl of cereal because they're still hungry," she says. If an hors d'oeuvre is served on a skewer or pick, Jean has practical advice. After parties she used to pull skewers out of every plant in her house. Now she cuts a lemon or orange in half, takes a tiny slice off the bottom so it doesn't slide, and places it on the tray so people have a place to stick the discarded skewers. And she advises that each skewer hold just one bite. "I remember when it was the fashion to spear three tortellini on one skewer," she says. "Well, after you eat the first one, then what do you do with it?"

Entertaining is getting very casual—more casual than a sophisticated hostess like Jean likes. But as beautiful as it can look, she advises, there's no need to serve a whole party with silver any longer. An assortment of trays and platters works well: silver, porcelain, and pretty ironstone are only a few possibilities. Trays should be simple, garnished with a little bunch of herbs, tiny flowers, or even parsley sprigs. "I always say that 'ten cents worth of parsley will cover up a multitude of sins,'" Jean says.

Toward the end of the evening, Jean will pass trays of sweets: tiny French brown-edge butter cookies and one-bite lemon or chocolate tarts. "After cocktails people crave a little something sweet," she says. "This is also a nice way of letting guests know the party's coming to an end; it's time to think about leaving."

How to Get the Most Out of a Cocktail Party

When you're the host:

    ❧ Even if you are expecting a crowd, prepare your home as carefully as you would for an intimate dinner party. Small bunches of flowers and votive candles (placed carefully so that guests will not accidentally tip them over) will provide touches of color and warmth.

ᴥ The host is the glue that holds the party together—especially at a cocktail party, where many people may be meeting for the first time. Realize that you are going to be "on" all night and give yourself time to relax before your guests arrive. Some hosts indulge in a "dressing drink"; some meditate. Plan ahead and do whatever it takes for you to feel party-ready.

ᴥ Don't let early birds throw you. Greet them warmly and say how glad you are to have them all to yourself for a moment. Instead of asking the staff to take coats or get drinks for early arrivals, do it yourself, chatting them up as you go. It will ease the strain of being the first guests and give you something to do.

ᴥ Try to stay close to the door in order to draw newcomers into the party. This may be a job that you share with a spouse; if you are entertaining solo, assign a friend or a staff member to help greet guests.

ᴥ Don't overwhelm guests with obtrusive music, especially in the early stages when you are afraid the party is too quiet. "Even when there are only a handful of guests, conversation is always the key to making people feel comfortable," says Michael Cannon, *Town & Country*'s editor-at-large and a frequent guest. "That's why I go to a cocktail party. If I wanted to listen to loud music, I could stay at home in my room with my headphones."

ᴥ As the party begins to wind down, people will feel awkward if they have to interrupt your conversation with other guests in order to offer their thanks. Keep yourself free so you can walk people to the door and say good night.

When you're a guest:

ᴥ Although your hosts may be trying to keep an eye on the door, by the time you arrive they may already be engaged in conversation with other guests. Seek them out to say hello *before* you get a drink.

ᴥ As Patrick Dennis's character Auntie Mame (in the film of the same name) instructed her nephew and "little love" Patrick, "Circulate, darling. Circulate." Say hello to the hosts upon entering, but don't monopolize them. Mingle and introduce yourself to other guests, keeping your conversation upbeat and respecting the difference between cocktail party chitchat and gossip. "There's such a thing as sincere small talk," says Michael Cannon. "You can always

87

OPPOSITE
**Fresh colorful garnishes
make functional and
attractive bar decorations.**

start a conversation by asking people about themselves."

❧ Even if you are only making a brief appearance, leave your coat and any work paraphernalia (like your briefcase) in the space provided. Walking around a party looking like someone who has one foot out the door makes other guests (not to mention your hosts) nervous.

❧ Don't assume that every kind of drink imaginable is being served. If the bar offerings are not obvious to you, ask the butler or bartender "Are you serving Manhattans tonight?" If the answer is no, don't insist that it's easy to make one. Simply say, "Okay, I'll have bourbon on the rocks."

❧ When it comes to hors d'oeuvre, if you are at a party where the waiter is trained to describe exactly what is on the tray, listen, decide, and take what is offered with your thanks, or say "No thank you" without any disclaimer (as in, "Oh, I would never eat duck"). Food commentary is not interesting or necessary.

❧ It is your responsibility to thank your hosts and say good night. They may or may not walk you to the door, but this is not the time to engage them in any conversation that keeps them from their other guests. Be gracious. Be brief. Be gone.

David Brown offers his expert advice on managing the business cocktail party.

All Business

DAVID BROWN

AFTER A LONG AND DISTINGUISHED CAREER as a theater and film producer (of such standouts as *Jaws*, *The Sting*, and *Driving Miss Daisy*), David Brown is veteran of who-knows-how-many cocktail parties. "When I was a very young journalist in the 1940s, I went to cocktail parties to meet women, and I still recommend the social cocktail party to single people as a dating venue. There is an element of the loss of control (within respectable limits) that can really be the start of something great," he says. "But in my earlier studio days I also learned that the office Christmas cocktail party could be the end of a career. People can make all kinds of mistakes empowered by alcohol."

Nowadays, any cocktail party David attends with his wife, Helen Gurley Brown, is strictly business, usually a "landmark" event—like a book party for a friend. "We pause outside the door, listening to the roar behind it. It can be terrifying to hear that cacophony of conversation," he says. "When I enter that room, I know I will be instantly enveloped by people I don't know, or people I am feverishly trying to avoid." So the couple arm themselves with David's hard-earned business party survival strategy, summed up in six easy steps:

The Brown Business Party Line

1. Arrive late. Cocktail parties are so crowded, who will know? As far as the host is concerned, you've been there all evening.

2. Try to focus on someone you know.

3. Stay near the exit.

4. Only take a drink when it is offered from a tray; fighting your way to the bar is too much work.

5. Never eat hors d'oeuvre; they just slow you down.

6. If it is an occasion of solemnity, try to figure out when the remarks (speeches and toasts) are being made and, just at the right moment, move closer to the people who are speaking. As soon as they are finished, head for the host and hostess, say your good-byes and gain credit for attending, then vaporize into the crowd, moving slowly toward the door, saying hello here and there on the way out.

Not Quite Christmas

CATHLEEN BLACK AND TOM HARVEY

ATHLEEN BLACK AND HER HUSBAND, Tom Harvey, host their annual holiday party during Thanksgiving week, a tradition that started when the couple lived in Washington, D.C., and continued after they moved to New York. People are already in a festive mood and looking forward to the holidays, but there's still a nice lull in those few days before Thanksgiving. "Later, in the season's crush of invitations, entertaining is so hectic that people can't even remember who is giving what party," explains Cathie, the president of Hearst Magazines.

Although Cathie's menu for an Indian-inspired cocktail supper may seem like a far-flung holiday choice, the spices typical of that cuisine (clove, cinnamon, allspice, nutmeg, and ginger) are also identified with the Christmas holidays without being overtly thematic. "I wanted to get away from the usual holiday fare. It's not what people expect," says Cathie, "but it still tastes and smells familiar."

Cathie continues the Indian-inspired theme with an uninhibited use of color in decorations. Her pale blue and green dining room is decorated in a French style, but for this party, she intensifies the look with rich colors and lush flowers, more free-form than formal. On the large oval buffet table, a centrally placed brass vase contains split and whole pomegranates, red roses, and

Tom Harvey and Cathleen Black prefer to host their annual holiday party early in the season.

evergreens, an exotic combination repeated in the fireplace mantel garland accented with ivory pillar candles and other small arrangements placed throughout the couple's home. The dining table, covered with a sage damask cloth, is decorated with ceramic elephants and scattered rose petals, and the food is served from rustic wooden platters, brass trays, and weathered wooden bowls, all resting on gold-colored raw silk mats. Hors d'oeuvre and desserts are passed on hammered brass chargers carried atop jewel-colored satin pillows—a dramatic touch that stops just short of being over-the-top.

"I never wanted to give a standard 'company holiday party.' I consider this time of the year an opportunity to mix friends and other publishing colleagues with those from the Hearst magazine family. At first, people were shocked to see so much food. But then I added the phrase 'cocktail supper' to the invitations, and now everyone has come to expect a meal."

With more than a hundred guests in attendance, the couple offer two full bars. An elongated apartment layout accommodates one in the library and a second in the family room, which helps to pull the crowd throughout the space. "But when I open the door at a party, I like to see a waiter standing there with a tray of prepoured wine and water, and so I also do that in my own home," Cathie says.

Although this is not a seated dinner, Cathie likes to keep the party structured. Toward the end of the evening (when guests begin to get restless), trays with bite-sized desserts (like brownies, blondies, thumbprint butter cookies, chocolate dipped pecans, and truffles) are passed, along with decaffeinated coffee in demitasse cups. "The dessert and coffee act as a signal to the guests that the party is nearing an end," she explains.

A Christmas Cocktail Party

THOMAS O'BRIEN

Seasonal party specialist Thomas O'Brien uses his Christmas tree as the center of the party's decorating theme.

THERE'S A FOUR-LETTER WORD to describe what happens when holiday enthusiasm meets a penchant for design: tree. Or, in the case of interior designer Thomas O'Brien, change that to enormous tree. Thomas, head of New York's Aero Studios and a major fan of holiday entertaining, is well known for his annual Christmas cocktail party, given every year without fail. "My friends have grown so accustomed to it, many use that party as a way to mark the season." Since Thomas's living room has an eighteen-foot ceiling, he puts up a larger-than-life tree, always decorated with special trimmings that vary

from holiday season to holiday season. "One year I covered the entire tree, top to bottom, with just silvery tinsel," says Thomas.

The tree decorations set the governing theme for the invitations, and Thomas takes pains to choose the perfect paper for the cards and envelope. The entire invitation is handwritten, not just the envelope. "I've done a pale gray card; another was a mixture of red and green stock on which I used white ink. Those cards reminded me of the photograph albums my mother kept when we were children—the photographs were mounted on black pages and she would write underneath each with white ink," he says.

The simple message "Come for Holiday Cocktails" is sent out to eighty guests. The guest list is a combination of good customers, referred to by Thomas as "friends of Aero," and people who work at design and interior magazines. But, in Thomas's mind, this is not a business party. Over the years, all the guests have gotten to know and like each other. "I don't invite people unless there's some kind of natural connection," he says. Because there are so many parties at that time of the year, Thomas extends the hours from the usual two-hour cocktail party to three hours so that guests who may be attending several events on the same night won't feel rushed on either end.

Thomas advises hosts to "circulate" in order to keep a party flowing.

92

With the tree taking center stage, other decorations tend to be low-key. "For the 'Year of the Tinsel,' I kept everything else light and fresh," Thomas explains, "using eucalyptus, berries, rose hips, and lots of white tulips on the mantel, flowers I consider very modern for the holidays. And since I love working with beautiful textiles, I draped the bar with pale green saris."

Instead of treating the bar like a utilitarian component, Thomas thinks of it as "a beautiful object," and is concerned with everything that guests will see, right down to the shape of the glasses and arrangement of the bottles. "I don't want the bottles lined up and looking like some 'speed rack' on a restaurant bar," he says. Glasses come from his own eclectic collection, gathered from a range of sources, whether antiques shops in London or junk shops in the country. When the guests come in, each picks a glass, which Thomas likens to "their own little identity."

The host extends the same careful consideration to stocking the bar, often tasting as many as five different white wines before settling on one to serve. In addition to white and red wine ("I don't emphasize it, but I do point out the red wine drinkers to the bartenders"), Thomas always serves champagne (Perrier-Jouet), and includes whiskey, vodka, and bourbon on the bar. "Bourbon and ginger ale, with lots of ice, is a popular drink at my house," he says. Thomas may also find a port or liqueur that he likes well enough to add to his bar offerings. "I think people appreciate a wonderful liqueur on a cold night, and it gives the bar a nice range."

Hosting a holiday party in a small apartment takes imagination, and Thomas uses every available bit of space. His midtown terrace has a view of both the Hudson and East Rivers, and Thomas rolls down the awning, lights votive candles, and places a stack of tartan blankets outside. "You'd be surprised how many guests go out there. It's cold but the view is worth it."

"It's hard to be a good host," Thomas concedes. "The most difficult part is making sure you greet people at the door." Once the party gets going, Thomas tends to the fire or passes an hors d'oeuvre tray. "Anything that keeps me moving around the party."

The Holiday Open House

ANYONE FAMILIAR with John Berendt's tale of the South, *Midnight in the Garden of Good and Evil*, knows about Jim Williams's legendary black-tie open house, "scheduled to occur at the climax of the Christmas season"—the party Savannah socialites once lived for. Butlers circulated with glasses of champagne on silver trays while guests nibbled cheese straws and marinated shrimp and tomato tea sandwiches from a buffet of low-country

food. Williams made it clear that he liked to reward or punish people by extending or withdrawing his invitation from year to year: "My out pile," he proclaimed, "is one inch thick."

Although this larger-than-life style of entertaining seems to belong to the South, no matter where you live, when you want to invite the most people your house can hold, it's time to throw an open house. Lacking the focused concentration of a dinner party, an open house is the perfect way to mix your various worlds (business associates, neighbors, friends, relatives, the young and old). And because people can come and go, it is most successful during the holiday season, when you are practically guaranteed that guests will have other things to do (which moves things along and helps control traffic).

It's easy to express the holiday spirit in the smallest of details.

The Pluses

&. The hours of an open house are flexible, ranging from late brunch and midday gatherings to early supper and nighttime parties.

&. Decorations and musical selections are a no-brainer. And if you're having trouble getting yourself ready for the holidays, having an open house will inspire you.

&. Crowded works. When a room is buzzing, you can forget about having the right number of chairs gathered around the dining room table and the perfect seating arrangement.

&. Themes work. What might be too informal (especially when entertaining business associates) becomes a lot of fun at the holidays:

tthe big deli-inspired spread or antipasto table, an all-day dessert banquet, the Southwestern chili and chips buffet.

 * You can follow through on your design without looking silly: Thematic paper napkins (and other disposable party supplies) or a less-than-full bar (just Mexican beer and pitchers of margaritas for the Southwestern party) don't look tasteless or thrifty at this time of the year. They look festive.

 * Service is flexible: No-fork food can be served buffet style with just a small plate or only a cocktail napkin.

 * Surprisingly, an open house is a great way to launch your hosting career. With a crowd in constant motion, the burden of carrying the conversational ball is not yours alone. Your biggest responsibility is "Hello," "Good-bye," and "Did you get enough to eat?"

 * When you host an annual open house, you not only create a tradition for your own family, but your party can become part of another family's holiday custom.

The Pitfalls

 * It is difficult to know how many guests you'll have. Although your invitations can be casual, it is still a good idea to add a response request. And since people may be coming from, or going to, other parties with a date, you might want to add the words "and guest."

 * Decide *in advance* if you want your open house to include young children. If so, add the words "and family" to the invitation. If you are aiming for an adults-only gathering, choose your party times accordingly. An invitation to an evening open house is not as child-friendly as an afternoon event.

 * Your biggest challenge as a host is keeping your open house fresh. Direct the staff to keep the surfaces in all the rooms free of food and drink debris, the glasses filled and the buffet looking its best. Nothing should look rundown to the new arrivals: not the food, not the bar, and especially not you.

 * Since there will always be a few guests who think an open house is an open-ended invitation and stay for the duration (causing a bottleneck), you may want to put a time restriction on invitations, staggering the hours for larger gatherings (for example, inviting half of the guests for four to seven and half for five to eight). Out with the old, in with the new is never more true than during a holiday open house.

Christmas, Southern Style

MIMI AND JOHN BOWEN

ALTHOUGH MIMI BOWEN and her husband, John, have been hosting an annual open house for eight years, there's still an element of surprise to the guest list. "A holiday open house gives me a chance to bring together people who wouldn't otherwise meet," says Mimi, the owner of a specialty jewelry and fashion shop in New Orleans. "I like to create an eclectic mix, not just my usual social set, and I randomly invite people I meet over the year, or those I don't get a chance to see often enough." The couple also ask their college-aged children to invite their friends, a nice addition to the party mix.

A custom-printed invitation, calling guests to "Holiday Cheer with Mimi and John Bowen," is sent out one month in advance. "I don't include a dress code because, around here, at Christmastime, it's a little like Mardi Gras," Mimi says. "No one needs to be reminded with a phrase like 'festive dress.'" Mimi also does away with a response request. "After eight years, I can't listen to all the phone messages anymore. Everybody knows which weekend the party is going to be, and they automatically hold the date."

When it comes to getting the couple's home party-ready, Mimi does the "whole Christmas deal": tree, flowers, and decorations. Inside, the house is traditionally centered around a thematic color scheme of red and gold. But Mimi always adds an outdoor decoration for every party—last year it was big

Mimi and John Bowen set the festive tone at their annual open house.

reindeer in the front yard. ("I'm afraid I'm going to have to stop soon. It is getting to look like Disneyland out there," she says.) Music plays a part in Mimi's plans as well—a continuous background of Christmas carols and other holiday standards. "But since I was born and raised in Memphis, it just wouldn't be Christmas without hearing Elvis sing how blue he'd be without me."

For the last several years, Mimi has used the same caterer for her party, and they "have it down to a science." Cocktail-napkin food, no plates. "I've learned to keep the menu the same. It's become a tradition," she says. "Whenever I try to change anything, people ask, 'Whatever happened to the so-and-so?'" The bar also stays the same: a full range of spirits, beer, wine, and champagne plus rental glasses in all the right shapes (martini, wine, double old-fashioned, and highball). "In the South, people enjoy whiskey-made drinks," Mimi says. With so many people and so much space, a double-bar in the sun room and single bars in the kitchen and music room keep things moving freely. Stations of food are strategically placed throughout the house, and Mimi instructs her caterer to keep them filled. One look at the menu and you'll understand why she says, "This has gotten to be such a great party that no one wants to leave, or, if they have to go to another party, they leave and come back."

101

The Bowen Family Christmas Open House Menu

ON THE KITCHEN TABLE
A Cajun Pirogue (*Oyster*) Station, including:
Baked Oysters (*on the half-shell*)
Oysters Cassis (*on a Stilton Cheese Cracker*)
Oysters Rockefeller (*with Spinach*)
Oysters Casino (*with Bacon and Parmesan*)
Oysters Bienville (*with Shrimp and Pimento*)

IN THE MUSIC ROOM
Smoked Salmon
with Garnishes, Mini Toasts, and Frozen Vodka

ON THE DINING ROOM TABLE
Crudités with Dips
Louisiana Gulf Shrimp
Deep-Fried Soft-Shell Buster Crabs and Crawfish
Mixed Grill
(*Andouille and Creole Sausage, Baby Lamb Chops, and Bite-Sized Alligator Bits*)

ON THE DINING ROOM SIDEBOARD
Assorted Desserts
(*Bite-Sized Brownies, Lemon Squares, Fruit Tarts, Cream Puffs, Chocolate-Dipped Strawberries, Sherried Pecans, and Chocolate Truffles*)

Classic Cocktails

THE TREND TOWARD RETRO-MODERN STYLE and design (so popular in the mid-fifties to early sixties) has created a renewed interest in everything "cocktail." Shakers, decanters, swizzle sticks, and other vintage hardware are collectibles, and a classic cocktail, straight up or on the rocks, has replaced the ubiquitous glass of cold white wine. Although the martini is the specialty drink most people choose for a cocktail party, other old standards have become "new" again.

Martini

Entire books have been devoted to this iconic cocktail. Possibly pioneered in the late 1870s under the name "Martinez," and certainly catapulted to fame by Ian Fleming's dashing character, James Bond (played so effectively by Sean Connery throughout the sixties and seventies in films like *Dr. No* and *Goldfinger*), the martini is a simple combination of gin and dry vermouth. It's the proportions that are complicated, and endless discussions take place over what constitutes a dry or extra-dry martini. Whatever your preferred ratio, the gin and dry vermouth are shaken (or stirred) with cracked ice and strained into a chilled cocktail glass, then garnished with an olive or twist of lemon peel.

Vodka Martini

The same as a martini but made with vodka (instead of gin) and dry vermouth.

Gibson

This (gin) martini garnished with pickled pearl onions was developed as a special drink for illustrator Charles Dana Gibson, creator of the turn-of-the-century "Gibson Girl," at the Players Club in New York City.

Manhattan

Usually made with bourbon (but it can be made with rye whiskey), sweet

Stocking the Bar

Even if you have a large home liquor inventory and an extensive range of mixers on hand (see Chapter Five, page 155), it is perfectly acceptable—advisable, really—to streamline your bar offerings at a cocktail party or open house. A good rule of thumb is that the larger the gathering, the more limited the selection. (This is the reason why bars at heavily attended events like art gallery openings offer only white wine and water.) There's no need for elaborate multiliquor concoctions, whirling blenders, and little paper drink umbrellas; you are hosting a party, not opening a nightclub. If you have light-colored furniture/rugs/floors and are reluctant to serve red wine and colored juices, then don't. (No excuses. No exceptions.) Most guests are perfectly happy to drink what is offered.

Although half-gallon bottles of spirits are economical, they're also unattractive, cumbersome, and can slow bartenders down, an important consideration at larger gatherings. Purchase spirits (and mixers) in one-liter bottles. Garnishes for drinks should be simple. Fresh lemon twists and lime wedges are all you need (plus whatever your specialty cocktails may require, like olives or maraschino cherries).

Beverages

A five-spirit bar, plus wine and mixers, works well for cocktail parties and open houses.

- Vodka, gin, scotch, blended whiskey, and bourbon (can be supplemented with rum in warmer weather or climates)
- Dry and sweet vermouth (these are sometimes called spirits, but they are actually fortified wines)
- Wine (red and white, or white only); you can also serve champagne
- Beer (a matter of seasonal and regional taste)
- Mixers (tonic, club soda, ginger ale, diet and regular cola; these can be supplemented with fruit juices)
- Water (flat and sparkling)

vermouth, and a touch of angostura bitters. This cocktail was invented at New York City's Manhattan Club in 1874 for a party given by Lady Randolph Churchill in honor of Governor Samuel J. Tilden, the lawyer who prosecuted members of the infamous "Boss" Tweed Ring.

Rob Roy
First cousin to the Manhattan, it's made with scotch and named after the legendary Scottish renegade hero.

Daiquiri
White rum, fresh lime juice, and sugar are combined in a cocktail named after the village of Daiquiri in Cuba. This famous drink, discovered by Teddy Roosevelt and the Rough Riders during the Spanish-American War, was immortalized by Ernest Hemingway at La Floridita (a bar in Havana nicknamed "Cradle of the Daiquiri"). It was John F. Kennedy's favorite cocktail before dinner.

Gimlet
A combination of gin and Rose's lime juice creates a cocktail with an eerie, pale greenish color. The preferred drink of Raymond Chandler's hard-boiled sleuth Philip Marlowe, the gimlet was celebrated as the cocktail that "beats martinis hollow" in *The Long Good-bye* (1953).

Sidecar
This mix of brandy, Triple Sec, and lemon juice, called the "expatriates' special," is rumored to have been first poured at Harry's Bar in Paris in the 1920s.

Stinger
White crème de menthe and brandy, rumored to be a great hangover cure, was claimed by writer Evelyn Waugh as his signature drink. In the 1956 film *High*

104

Society, C. K. Dexter-Haven (Bing Crosby) offers one to a hungover Traci Lord (played by Grace Kelly) with this promise: "It's a stinger. It removes the sting."

Old-Fashioned

Sugar and bitters muddled with a slice of orange and layered with bourbon (or rye) and lots of ice in its namesake glass. The first old-fashioned was served at the Pendennis Club in Louisville, Kentucky, in the late 1880s.

Tom Collins

The Singapore sling–like concoction of gin, lemon juice, sugar, and soda water that was originally made in the late 1800s with sweet gin called Old Tom. It is served in its namesake glass.

Placing and Boxing the Bar

Since cocktail parties are often crowded, a bar should be placed where it can accommodate the most people in the least amount of space. Not even party professionals can tell you exactly where that spot is until they see your home. If you are working with a new caterer, this means a site visit before making any plans concerning placement.

Once the bar is placed, it should be covered with a cloth, not just to protect the surface of the table being used but to hide anything being stored under the table. Unlike a cloth draped over a table at a seated party (and allowed to fall in luxurious folds), a professional catering staff has a technique for "boxing" a standard-size rental table with its matching cloth. By using a few angular folds (that pull the tablecloth taut and hold it in place without sliding), they can create a neat, straight-sided "box," with the table covered (to the floor) on three sides and the open side facing the bartender (for access to the storage space). Icing tubs and supplies are placed on plastic or carpet bar mats to protect the floor from spills and scratches.

Basic Barware

Classic cocktails call for just the right glasses.

ALTHOUGH THE ENTERTAINING TREND leans toward the use of all-purpose glasses, there is a proper glass for every cocktail, and most rental companies stock a variety of classic shapes (see Chapter Five, page 157). A glass is considered to be an important part of a drink (in terms of how it looks and how it feels in your hand), and serving drinks in the wrong one can be interpreted as a sign of an inexperienced bartender. But since anticipating how many of each shape will be needed (without rewashing) over the course of a two-hour cocktail party is difficult (and potentially expensive, since many glasses can go unused), it is understandable to limit the variety of glasses used at larger home gatherings. More important than the shape of the glass is the size: two ounces of scotch in a ten-ounce glass isn't going to work, no matter how much ice you add. If you need to limit, settle for one all-purpose stemware glass (for wine, water, and highballs), an old-fashioned glass (for spirits on the rocks) and the specific glass required for any specialty cocktail being served (like martinis).

Cocktail (also called a martini glass)

Three- to ten-ounce stemmed glass; the four- to six-ounce range is most practical.

Highball

Eight- to ten-ounce tumbler in different shapes (can be wider in the middle or at the bottom), traditionally used for liquor and water or effervescent mixers.

Collins

Ten- to fourteen-ounce chimney-shaped glass (narrow, with straight sides), for Tom Collins and juice drinks (like Cape Cod); can be used interchangeably with highball glass in the home bar.

Old-fashioned (also called a lowball, whiskey, or rocks glass)

Four- to eight-ounce short tumbler that can be used for any cocktail served "on the rocks."

All-purpose

Ten- to twelve-ounce stemware good for wine (even champagne), water, soda; can be used interchangeably with the highball glass in the home bar.

What to Say to a Naysayer

With the renewed interest in cocktail parties, it only follows that some of the old criticisms have resurfaced as well. Here is a guide to separating the facts from the fiction behind the most common cocktail party complaints.

People only throw cocktail parties because they're less expensive than other kinds of parties.

Not true. There's more to a cocktail party than you can see from the vantage point of being a guest. When you figure the expense of stocking the bar and renting glasses, add in the caterer and extensive staff required (kitchen workers, butlers, bartenders), a cocktail party can be more costly than a buffet.

People only throw cocktail parties because they're "paybacks."

Often true, but so what? People with limited space and time may want to entertain more people than they can seat at their table, and the cocktail party is a great way to make that happen.

Cocktail parties are crowded and noisy.

True, but understandable. There's a parable about a turtle and a scorpion: After transporting the scorpion across a river on its back, the turtle gets stung and cries out, "Why did you do that?" To which the scorpion philosophically replies, "It's just my nature." So it goes: The cocktail party, with its raucous speakeasy roots, can't help being what it is. Mixing lots of people with alcohol in rooms that seem too small may not be your idea of a perfect time, but there is something deadly about too few people in rooms that are too large—that's a party that never got off the ground.

You never get a chance to have a "real conversation."

True, but what's the harm? A cocktail party is not intended as a place for intense conversation. Cocktail parties are not about a full meal in any sense of the word; they're about the "nibble": an hors d'oeuvre here, a snippet of conversation there. You might even be able to find a quiet corner.

The food is so fattening (at least the good food is).

True, but avoidable. Cocktail parties aren't about nutrition, and no one should attend a cocktail party for health. When considering the menu, the key words for a host have always been "tiny, crispy, crunchy, salty, and cheesy." For a guest, "No thank you."

CHAPTER 4

Outdoor Entertaining

ITHOUT A WELL-THOUGHT-OUT alfresco dining area equipped to accommodate guests, outdoor entertaining can lead to extreme measures. In the 1989 film adaptation of Robert Harling's engaging play *Steel Magnolias*, an aggravated host decides to shoot a flock of bothersome birds out of the trees before a backyard luncheon. Others, who consider entertaining outdoors as an option for special occasions only, can incur enormous expense—like the overwhelmed father who listens incredulously as a party planner suggests renting swans to accessorize his daughter's lavish tented wedding in the 1991 remake of that sentimental fifties film classic *Father of the Bride*. Perhaps you won't find yourself in such theatrical predicaments, but any host considering alfresco entertaining should be warned: Successful outdoor parties take more than planning. They also require the right props.

From dancing under the trees to dinners on the deck, it only takes a little extra planning and the right kind of weather for any party to move successfully outdoors. And when you're especially lucky, add a big mellow moon and a sky full of stars.

California Cuisine

KIM AND MICHAEL McCARTY

For Michael McCarty, owner of Michael's restaurants in Santa Monica and New York, and his wife, Kim, outdoor entertaining in their Malibu, California, home is simply a way of life. Kim and Michael's home was designed as an indoor-outdoor house, not just for the wraparound redwood decks that afford spectacular views of the Pacific—and of Michael's two-and-a-half-acre vineyard—but also for the relationship of the spaces.

The couple's enthusiasm for entertaining has inspired three kitchens: the main one, located indoors (with ample counter space and ovens); a second "back kitchen" (with workhorse equipment like dishwashers); and the outdoor cooking areas, outfitted with a Viking grill and wood-burning oven. Adjacent to the central dining deck, a glass-walled room designed to give the illusion of continuous space serves as a lounge, where people often have drinks from a full bar before dinner. "I like to move from one space to another for each distinct segment of the evening," says Michael.

California's balmy climate permits the McCartys to entertain outdoors almost year round. Although guests expect to be dining alfresco, invitations still include a reminder so people will come prepared, especially when the deck is being used in cooler weather. The couple also keeps a collection of shawls, jackets, and sweaters on hand, "just in case."

Michael doesn't work from a seating chart or use place cards. Rather, he seats everyone himself, often deciding at the last minute. For small parties, he uses a rectangular table that can seat six to eight; for larger gatherings, folding tables can extend seating capability to forty guests. During the day, the main table is sheltered by a big canvas umbrella that provides shade, as well as dramatic

An exuberant Michael McCarty prepares for lunch alfresco.

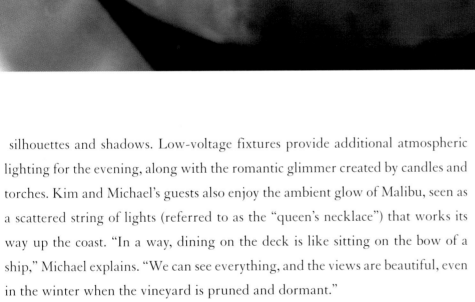

silhouettes and shadows. Low-voltage fixtures provide additional atmospheric lighting for the evening, along with the romantic glimmer created by candles and torches. Kim and Michael's guests also enjoy the ambient glow of Malibu, seen as a scattered string of lights (referred to as the "queen's necklace") that works its way up the coast. "In a way, dining on the deck is like sitting on the bow of a ship," Michael explains. "We can see everything, and the views are beautiful, even in the winter when the vineyard is pruned and dormant."

"We are lucky to live in a part of the country where we are not bothered by mosquitoes, a real deterrent to eating outdoors," he continues. At the height of the season, when the grapes in the neighboring vineyard are loaded with sugar, they may get swarms of bees, "but the bees always seem to prefer the grapes to the guests."

To set the table, Michael and Kim use the "real stuff." Place mats may be acceptable for afternoon parties, but tablecloths are de rigueur for the evening. The hosts favor all-white linens, including extra-generous napkins (twenty-seven inches square), and oversized white brasserie plates. This frees them to use the food and the flowers for color on the table. Decorations lean toward small accent flowers on the tables, while larger arrangements are used for impact throughout the house.

Two Malibu Menus

Summer
Brunch Alfresco

Blood Orange Mimosa

**Vine-Ripened Heirloom Tomatoes
with Mozzarella, Basil, and Walla Walla
Sweet Onions**

**Grilled Wild Alaskan Sockeye Salmon
with Meyer Lemon and Thyme**

**Succotash of Sautéed White Corn,
Fava Beans, Fingerling Potatoes,
and Shiitake Mushrooms**

Parma Prosciutto and Melon des Cavaillere

Arugula, Fennel, and Parmesan Salad

Fraises des bois with *Fromage Blanc*

WINES
**Chardonnay and Pinot Noir
(*Malibu Vineyards*)**

Winter
An Evening Outdoors

Pacific Northwest Oysters on the Half-Shell

**Seared Hudson Valley Duck Foie Gras
on Walnut Toast**

**Grilled Channel Island Lobsters
with Basil Garlic Butter**

Warm Wild Mushroom and Pine Nut Salad

**Lamb Chops with Rosemary Potatoes
and Haricot Vert**

**Cookies with Caramel, Vanilla,
and Coffee Ice Cream**

Espresso

WINES
**Chardonnay, Cabernet Sauvignon, Merlot,
and Cabernet Franc Blend
(*Malibu Vineyards*)**

Kim (a painter whose work hangs in the McCarty home and both restaurants) is particularly adept at mixing the colors and shapes of flowers and branches used in the arrangements. The food, often presented family style for guests to pass around, serving themselves, makes up the rest of the table decoration.

Although the McCartys' favorite hors d'oeuvre are assorted caviar, smoked salmon, raw oysters, and seared foie gras, the main course is likely to be a simple combination of the best ingredients the season has to offer. Michael does the cooking himself, although for larger parties he brings in a crew from his restaurant to work with him. When the guest list reaches twenty-four, the hosts may shift from the usual family-style service to buffet or even plated service, depending on the menu. What doesn't change is Michael's insistence on the big bold flavors of the California-style cuisine he is famous for helping to introduce to the rest of the country. "I never know what I'm going to serve until I go to the market. Then I see what is fresh," he says. "We take advantage of what nature has to offer."

Forces of Nature

W HEN IT COMES TO ENTERTAINING OUTDOORS, three things can always foil alfresco dining: bugs, insufficient lighting, and bad weather.

What's the Buzz?

Ask anyone who's ever tried to hold a drink in one hand and swat bugs with other other: Living with mosquitoes (and other biting insects) is no party. At some point your guests must move indoors, or the mosquitoes must move away from your guests. To reduce mosquito activity:

ᔏ Eliminate standing water from around the party area: birdbaths, puddles under leaky faucets, saucers under potted plants, and the bottom of any open grill. (The chlorine in swimming pools usually prevents mosquitoes from gathering.)

ᔏ Use an area repellent spray (also known as a fogger) several hours before guests arrive.

ᔏ Surround the party area with natural repellents like citronella (available in candles and essential oil for torches and outdoor lanterns) or cedar coils that attack the mosquitoes' sense of smell. However, be warned that once you are standing outside the plume of smoke, mosquitoes will usually return.

ᔏ Keep any platters of food covered with mesh domes until you're ready to eat.

ᔏ Stock up on a variety of spray-on bug blockers. Whether your guests want to use them or not is up to them.

ᔏ Consider electronic mosquito repelling devices that offer protection without creating too much noise.

ᔏ Bear in mind that mosquitoes intensify around dusk. You may want to have drinks outside and move inside as the sun begins to set, or wait until it's dark to move outside and eat.

The right outdoor lighting can make an evening glow longer.

Here Comes the Night

Groping for your silverware as darkness descends is not only uncomfortable, it's dangerous. Here's how to design a safe lighting plan and turn your backyard into an intimate nighttime hideaway:

ᔏ Choose low-voltage deck lights to define steps, railings, and deck posts and landscape lights to highlight trees, gardens, and architectural features. Path lights will keep walkways and access routes visible.

ᔏ Use decorative outdoor electric lanterns (post, hanging, and wall mounted) to cast an illuminating glow on patios and terraces.

ᔏ To spread lights though a larger area, try tiny white Christmas tree lights (available in basic strings or "nets," typically used to cover shrubs and bushes) and decorative lanterns (like globes or whimsical shapes like dragonflies)

designed to cover a strand of light bulbs. Sturdy oil torches can also be used to highlight gardens and walkways.

🦋 Add accent lights with candles, choosing votives in protective holders or tapers/pillars with glass hurricane shades; they prolong burning time and prevent accidents.

🦋 Rice paper lanterns (that fit over bulbs), available in every imaginable color, can be strung from trees or bamboo poles for an East-meets-West look.

The Sky Is Falling

No matter how well prepared or superbly organized you may be, inclement weather can make it impossible to go forward with your outdoor entertaining plans. Retractable canvas awnings and canopies (that shelter without enclosing) can supply relief-on-demand from a sudden shower, but nothing can save your party from prolonged rain or strong winds. Even supplying a rain date isn't practical; the weather can change suddenly on the day of the party.

Although you can always convert an outdoor party into a casual one indoors, when formal dining is on your agenda, there is only one practical solution: Don't invite more guests than you can accommodate with indoor seating.

Patricia Cook puts the finishing touches on one of her fantasy table settings.

Where the Living Is Easy

PATRICIA COOK

PATRICIA COOK, who likes to say she's gone "from Mississippi to Moscow with some amazing stops along the way," splits her year between England and Palm Beach. Although she admits that the entertaining she does in England is "quite a different thing," when Florida rolls out the good-weather welcome, Patricia responds with a series of seated parties in her Palm Beach home "geared for eating outdoors."

Unless it is a special occasion, like a birthday or anniversary, Patricia dispenses with printed invitations and just picks up the telephone. "I don't have to tell people we'll be eating outdoors. They expect it," she says. Seating arrangements on her patio are centered around a large glass-topped table. ("It's too heavy to move.") Depending on the mood she is trying to establish, she seats eight to twelve at that table, and another twenty to thirty at round

folding tables. Although the tables are semiprotected by canvas umbrellas, Patricia has a simple contingency plan in mind for inclement weather: She asks her guests to pick up everything and move into the house. "I don't worry about having too many guests and too few seats. Maybe it has something to do with being from the South, but I like these spur-of-the-moment changes; they can keep things a little more relaxed."

Patricia is one hostess who likes to use place cards. Without them, she maintains, seating a table can be a little like playing hide-and-seek. When she is "feeling subtle" and doesn't want to add to the decorative scheme of the table, she uses a plain engraved card. But sometimes she likes to tie the place card to the look of the table, and claims, "I've done it all, from writing on leaves to using wine cords as holders."

Drinks are served from a full bar before dinner, and Patricia favors light food during the cocktail hour. "I used to serve a whole range of hors d'oeuvre, but over the years I've come to feel like an overprotective parent does toward a

By setting up the buffet in the house and seating on the terrace, Patricia allows her guests to enjoy the best of both worlds.

To plan the menus, Patricia Cook joins forces with her cook, Ruby Princess. "We're a good match," she explains. "Ruby is creative with cuisine, treating the food as I do flowers. We are both directly inspired by what looks good in the market. I trust her instincts. She will often come to me and say, 'There are wonderful stone crabs,' or 'the artichokes look good right now.' Then we take it from there."

Island Evening

❦

Fried Okra Salad

Jamaican Jerk Chicken with Banana Ketchup and Guava Sauce

Black Beans, Yellow Rice, and Stir-Fry Vegetables

Frozen Margarita Pie with Pretzel Crust

Palm Beach Barbecue

❦

Grilled Vegetable Gazpacho

Baby Back Ribs and Chicken with Papaya Barbecue Sauce

Scallion Spoonbread

Yukon Gold Potato Pie

Ginger Plum Cake

HOUSE DRINKS
Rum and Ginger Ale with Fresh Sugar Cane and Mint

Rum Slush with Mango Purée and Pineapple Juice

OPPOSITE
Emphasize the outdoors by incorporating natural elements into the table settings.

child: I don't want my guests to spoil their lovely dinner," she says. And since it can be impossible to balance a drink, eat, and talk at the same time, Patricia offers her guests what she considers to be easy-to-manage "nibbly" food: crudités, almonds, and popcorn, because "women will eat it without feeling guilty."

Once the framework of the party is complete, Patricia can do what she does best: create an environment with flowers, fabric, and table settings. "I'm a frustrated set designer to the core," she admits. "I work and work on a party until I get it to look the way I want it to look." Patricia is an ardent and inventive collector, whose cache of linens, crystal, and china resembles a theatrical company's prop closet. "I have a real hunting-and-gathering mentality and I find fun, funky pieces when I'm traveling," she says. Patricia likes to see an unexpected variety of colors and shapes on the table, including unusual containers for flowers, from wooden wine boxes, watering cans, and oversized shells to an odd assortment of wicker fishing creels. One of her all-time favorite settings was a hollowed-out, greenish-purple gourd filled with blue-green lisianthus, lilac hyacinths, and cream roses on a Degas-green moiré tablecloth.

Although Patricia, the recipient of several awards from the Palm Beach Garden Club, enjoys the look of roses, tulips, and lilies, her interest does not end with cultivated flowers. "My mother and grandmother were passionate gardeners, and I grew up with an appreciation of garden flowers, like Queen Anne's lace, anemones, delphinium, and sweet peas," she says. She also stays open to all the possibilities nature has to offer, and loves the earthy charm of moss, weeds, rocks, flowering branches, and vines. "There's even a drama in using stems and stalks of vegetables, like green bean blossoms. They add another dimension to your table."

Decorating Alfresco

OUTDOOR ENTERTAINING can mean augmenting your usual flower selections with greenery to give your table a polished but natural look and feel.

🌿 Formal floral arrangements can seem out of place in a natural setting, and delicate flowers that flourish in air-conditioned rooms can suddenly wilt in outdoor heat. Landscape your table with pots of blooming herbs (rosemary, elderberry, and lavender) and wheat grass planted in color-washed wooden or weathered metal boxes.

🌿 Choose decorative elements that harmonize with your surroundings: twig place mats, sea grass baskets, glazed ceramic and clay pots, in shades ranging from emerald green to ruddy-colored terra-cotta.

🌿 Even in arid areas, take advantage of dramatic natural scenery by combining potted cacti and other succulents (like *Echeveria* "Afterglow" and "Violet Queen") with table decorations created from natural materials like leather, horn, and wood.

🌿 Enchant the wandering eye: drape garden statuary with floral or leaf garlands, and outline trellises (along with other architectural detailing) in twinkling lights.

Creature Comforts

Outdoor entertaining can be less formal than the parties you give inside your home, but attention to all the little details is still required to put your guests at ease.

🌿 Use clamps or clip-on weights (both available at most hardware and gardening stores) to keep tablecloths from blowing in the wind.

🌿 Make sure the surfaces (especially edges) of outdoor furniture (like rattan, wicker, rough-hewn wood, painted wrought iron) are splinter and snag proof, without sharp or protruding pieces.

🌿 For safe footing, tiles used for the patio (especially the dining area) should be textured (not smooth) to prevent slipping, and since high heels have a way of getting caught in the separations between planking on wooden decks, check to see that the boards under and around the dining table are closely aligned.

🌿 Tables should be placed directly on the lawn only where the ground is dry, firm, and level.

CHAPTER **5**
The Grand Scheme

YOU PLAN, you work, you worry—so why would you want your party to be anything less than a singular sensation? The truth is that all parties—at least all good parties—have something in common: structure. Whether you are hosting a black-tie dinner in town or a country-style open house, success depends on a functional framework. Planning a party is a lot like building a house: both require a strong foundation, top-quality materials, and the expertise of well-chosen professionals.

Caterers

AS A HOST, you will be called upon to make decisions that shape your party long before invitations are delivered. Among the most important is finding the right private caterer, an expert in the highly specialized world of home entertaining whose job description falls somewhere between an event planner (who might coordinate a wedding) and the chef at your favorite restaurant.

Finding a Caterer

The most efficient way to get the name of a good caterer is through referral, but even a glowing recommendation from your most trusted friend won't guarantee a successful working relationship. The personal service offered by a private caterer consists of much more than the exchange of food and money. Caterers have diverse skills as well as different personalities. Use the same criteria you would in evaluating any other relationship: You and your caterer should have common goals and mutual attraction. Hire a caterer who shares your point of view about entertaining, someone you *like*, and build a lasting collaboration from there.

A trickier situation occurs when you discover a caterer while attending a party in someone else's home (instead of through direct referral). No matter how impressed you are, curb any impulse to blurt out "Who did the catering?" Inquiring about the caterer during a party takes the spotlight off the hosts by

minimizing the importance of their role. It's like saying "What a gorgeous room! Who's your decorator?" Instead, telephone the host with your thanks and single out some detail that was uniquely their contribution (for example, the wonderfully varied guest list) before complimenting the food and asking if they would share the telephone number of their caterer. Don't be surprised if they politely decline. When it comes to personal services, some people are reluctant to share resources.

There is also a practical reason why trying to meet caterers during parties is awkward: They should not come out of the kitchen, and guests should not go in. Nor should any member of the caterer's staff produce a business card, even if asked. (You certainly don't want a caterer passing out business cards in *your* home.) The proper response from a butler is to furnish the caterer's name (on request), adding that the telephone number is available from the host. And if the host doesn't want to share, well, at least you have a name.

Getting Started

Once you have a caterer in mind, the first step is to arrange to meet in your home as far in advance of your party date as your social calendar and the caterer's booking schedule permits. This initial visit should address both practical concerns and aesthetic considerations, ranging from the working efficiency of your kitchen, including the quality and assortment of cooking equipment, to your color preferences and overall sense of style. It is important for the caterer to see your china (both formal and informal) so menus can be designed with the size and pattern of the plates in mind. Give the caterer a tour of the rooms the guests will be using—not just the kitchen and dining room—so he or she can become familiar with the personal touches that distinguish your home (and your parties) from those of other clients. Since the best entertaining is individualistic, any caterer worth keeping must understand that regardless of food fads or entertaining trends, the only style that really matters to you is your own.

Although caterers can seem like magicians when it comes to creating parties, they are not clairvoyant. You have to tell them what you want. Broadly outline your ideal party from menu to atmosphere and let the professional help crystallize your ideas, bearing in mind real-life considerations like the space and equipment limitations of your kitchen and how traffic flows in your entertaining areas. Listen carefully to advice: An innovative caterer can give you a whole new party perspective by using your home in ways you've never imagined.

Other Services the Caterer Provides

During your first meeting, ask any questions you may have about the range of the caterer's services that you can expect from him or her. Most caterers who specialize in home entertaining have no set policy, preferring instead to accommodate each client individually. A caterer can arrange for staff to arrive in time to take care of everything from polishing silver to arranging flowers, or the staff can arrive to a table that has already been set, right down to place cards, by the client. Naturally, all variations in service are reflected in price.

Settle Money Issues Right Away

Take advantage of the initial meeting to discuss billing procedures, fee structures, and staffing estimates. Most caterers use a simple formula: a 30 to 50 percent working deposit, with the balance due within two weeks following the party. While the set staffing fees are billed on the food invoice, gratuities are customarily presented (preferably in cash), at your discretion, directly to individual staff members at the party's end. If the caterer is arranging for COD deliveries (for rental equipment, for example), an itemized list of the expenses should be provided at least two days before the party so you have ample time to write checks.

Maintaining Consistency

Since many caterers who specialize in home entertaining run small, boutiquelike businesses and are loyal to repeat clients, ask if you can expect to see the caterer personally at *your* party. When schedule conflicts do occur, will you meet their second-in-command well before the event? Can the caterer send staff members who are familiar with the workings of your home so you don't have to start all over again at each party? If you want to join the circle of regular clients, check your entertaining schedule in advance, especially during the holidays, and give the caterer hold dates along with deposits.

This is also the perfect time to ask the caterer how the staff will be dressed: Are there different uniforms for different occasions? For example, butlers wearing simple attire (like white shirt, black vest, and a black tie) are better suited to an informal gathering than a staff dressed in tuxedoes.

Planning a Menu

Planning a menu with caterers who offer this sort of personal service may take longer than with those who limit choices to selections from set menus and "party packages." When you are paying for this individual attention, take advantage of it. Why open a menu discussion by describing each and every dish your friend's caterer served? Instead of duplicating someone else's party, allow your caterer to design a proposal just for you. If the party proposal is attached to a fee structure that you are not prepared to meet, ask the caterer to suggest options so you can decide where to cut or splurge. And if the caterer's menu doesn't reflect your intention for the party, trust your taste enough to make suggestions of your own. It helps to understand that the caterer cannot make the price lower by reducing the portions. Running out of hors d'oeuvre or not being able to serve seconds defeats the purpose of having a party and is not the way to save money.

If you have a specific budget in mind, tell the caterer the exact amount you want to spend so he or she can tailor the menu to the money. That's another advantage of a long-term relationship: Your caterer comes to understand and accommodate the full (price) range of your entertaining needs.

Don't Skimp on Staff

Most caterers will tell you that the biggest mistake clients make is assuming that the more staff members present, the more formal the party will feel. But it

Who's Who

Most caterers who specialize in home entertaining pride themselves on assembling a graciously accommodating crew who are as responsive to requests as your own household staff would be. No, they won't wash your windows and walk your dog, but you certainly won't encounter a "that's not my job" attitude when you ask someone to perform a task that falls into a coworker's territory. Although uniformly dressed and accustomed to multitasking, here's a general outline of what each member of a catering crew does, and how their jobs may be defined on a staffing estimate and/or invoice.

Headwaiter (or Captain)
The headwaiter is in charge of the party, coordinating service in the kitchen and in the dining room, as well as answering any questions the hosts may have.

Butlers
Even though they are responsible for serving food and drinks, these staff members are not typically referred to as waiters because they also perform some of the same functions as would private household staff: answering the door and greeting guests, taking coats, and handling the telephone (including taking any messages) during the party.

Bartenders
Although they may be pressed into food service during seated dinner parties (as guests move into the dining area and bar service slows down), bartenders are usually designated to handle beverages (mixing drinks and pouring wine) during the cocktail hour. At cocktail parties and during an open house, tending bar is typically their sole function.

Runners
Although they may also perform kitchen duties (handling rental equipment, for example), a food runner's main responsibility is to replenish the buffet, making the trip between the kitchen and the dining area so the butlers who are serving the guests do not have to leave their stations. A staff member who provides the same service for bartenders (replenishing beverages and restocking ice and glassware) is called a bar runner, or bar back.

Many hosts request the same staff for their parties, and as result are on a first-name basis with their regular butlers and bartenders. For first-time hosts (or when the staff is larger than usual), take the time to learn each staff member's name before the party begins. It is a nice gesture for the host to turn to a guest and say, "Here, let Tom take your coat," or ask a butler, "Gary, could you bring Mrs. Kaye a drink?"

doesn't matter whether it was a frankfurter or filet mignon on the plates; they still need to be washed.

To provide the level of service that you should expect in your home (and to return that home to mint condition), a caterer will allocate one butler for every eight guests at a seated dinner; one butler for every twelve guests at a buffet; and one butler for every fifteen guests at a cocktail party. The number of food runners and kitchen staff will vary according to menu, efficiency of your kitchen, extent of clean-up (rental place settings and stemware can be returned without being washed—not true of your own china and glassware), and how the meal is served. Just because you are having a buffet doesn't mean the food serves itself. A buffet table is usually manned by two staff members, with additional butlers on hand to look after guests, plus food runners to keep the table replenished; all of these are in addition to the kitchen staff. Bartenders constitute another variable, and staffing them is determined not only by the number of guests but also by the style of the bar: serving a full bar (mixed drinks in addition to wine) will double the number of bartenders needed at anything but the most intimate gathering.

Most caterers use a headwaiter to oversee service to guests while they concentrate on the kitchen duties. The caterer often leaves a party after dessert is served, relying on the headwaiter to "book out" by supervising clean-up (including repacking any rental equipment), tallying wages, and making sure you are satisfied. When your own china and glassware are used, the headwaiter may ask you to check it before releasing the staff. When a dish or glass has been broken, the headwaiter usually shows it to you at the party's end and extends the offer to pay for repair or replacement. (Whether you accept that offer or not depends entirely on you; just remember that accidents are bound to happen, even with the most conscientious staff.) Due to his additional responsibilities, the headwaiter is always billed at a higher rate than other staff, and he is tipped accordingly.

Mixing your own household staff with the caterer's is not a constructive way to cut costs. Catering in a private home is a very specific skill; caterers simply cannot direct in-house staff as effectively as they can their own employees. Although the caterer's staff may move around in a deceptively casual manner, they have the well-coordinated "body knowledge" of people accustomed to working together in small spaces and should be free to do their jobs without interference from household employees, who may become territorial, especially in the kitchen.

Do It or Delegate It

Catering is loaded with boring details and trivialities: silver polish, paper towels, coat hangers. If you plan ahead, caterers can arrange to provide everything. But if you tell them that you or your housekeeper will get these things, they should be available when the caterer arrives. Timing is critical during setup, and a caterer's least favorite preparty scenario is taking a staff member away from basic duties to run household errands.

On the day of the party, it is essential that your household staff be finished with their chores by the time the caterer arrives. This is particularly true of anything that interferes with setup, like waxing the kitchen floor while the staff is trying to unload or ironing linens needed to set the table. Arrange for young children (and their baby-sitter) to be fed somewhere other than the kitchen by someone other than the caterer and banish even the most pampered pets to another part of the house (for their own safety).

With kitchen space at a premium, plan for all necessary deliveries, such as liquor, to arrive the day before the party. If you are using a floral designer, he or she must be finished with the work, include cleaning, by the time the catering staff arrives. Caterers and florists need the same counter and sink space, and it pays to remember that olive oil and water do not mix.

Get Your Kitchen into Shape for a Party

Clear off counters, empty the dishwasher, take all those extra pans out of the oven and maximize refrigerator space. When using your own place settings, make sure the catering staff understands what goes into the dishwasher and what needs to be hand-washed—such as delicate or hand-painted china and porcelain, silver, crystal, antiques, anything with silver or gold trim, and utensils with bone or

handles. Provide lint-free drying cloths (linen or absorbent huck toweling is best) and stacking liners for plates (felt, cloth, even paper towels will do).

If you entertain regularly, have your oven calibrated and install a thermometer for accurate readings. The oven should also be clean and the exhaust fan operational. Have several different-sized vases handy for that inevitable moment when a guest arrives carrying cut flowers, and set aside a room where the catering staff can change and store their bags.

Be a Great Communicator

After you're finished dressing, but before the guests arrive, take the time to have a service meeting with the entire staff. Let the butlers know how you would like them to answer the door. Clearly describe how you see the party going, from where coats belong to the surprise toast you are planning to give just before dessert. Anticipate a general timeline—for example, if guests are coming for drinks at seven-thirty, let the caterer know you are expecting to serve dinner at eight-fifteen. If the caterer cannot see the dining room from the kitchen, keep the headwaiter posted if changes occur so that he can make the necessary time adjustment for the food.

Respect Your Caterer's Space

Coming into the kitchen while the caterer is working is like going backstage during a performance: It's a privilege. There is no way the caterer can stop your friend, the foodie, from standing dangerously close to the stove at just the wrong moment while confiding "I just love to cook." But *you* can. Make telephones in other rooms available for guest use. And designate a separate area for smokers, or they'll end up congregating in the kitchen.

Tell Your Caterer the Truth

When something goes wrong, say so immediately. You're not doing any favors by overlooking the problem, no matter how trivial it may seem. It is your caterer's business to know exactly what does and doesn't work for you. Only then do you stand a chance of becoming a real working team.

Invitations

ALTHOUGH TELEPHONE INVITATIONS may work for smaller parties, once your guest list exceeds the number that can be seated in your dining room, it is better to send a written one. A written invitation doesn't just set forth the details of a party, it can establish the tone, acting as a precursor of what is to come—the pomp that precedes the circumstance. "I always send an invitation," says New York fashion designer James Mischka of Badgley Mischka. "It's proper. It shows you've made an effort." Written invitations also have the built-in bonus of acting as a tangible reminder for your guests.

Spreading the Word

For smaller (a cocktail party that doesn't exceed the comfort level of your living room, for example) or semiformal parties, invitations should be mailed in time for guests to receive them at least two weeks before the gathering. For larger or more formal events, and certainly any parties during the busy holiday season, it is practical to allow three to four weeks. (Remember, this is not a timetable for mailing the invitations; this is the schedule for receiving them.) To help guarantee a good turnout during the holidays, telephone your guests with a hold date and follow up with the written invitation.

Form and Function

In private life, formally worded engraved invitations are reserved for the largest and most special of parties: momentous occasions like a significant anniversary or birthday. The next level of formality is the custom-printed invitation, available through the stationery department of better department stores and at specialty stationers. While custom-printing may not require as much lead time as engraving, advance arrangements are still necessary. You need to make an appointment with a sales consultant, who will advise you on the style and wording of the invitation before furnishing a proof (or facsimile) of the invitation, which can take two weeks. After checking the proof carefully and finalizing your order, expect delivery of the completed invitations to take another two to four weeks. Since invitations to any party in your home should be addressed by hand, make arrangements for the envelopes to be sent immediately (including several extra) so that you can work through the guest list at your leisure. For small dinners and other intimate gatherings, use high-quality, fill-in-the-blank invitations (the design motif should match the occasion) or your own personalized note cards.

The simplest invitation is usually the most sophisticated, and you can never go wrong with a traditional approach. However, there are times when something stylized and distinctive (like vintage black-and-white postcards) can be used to create a unique look. In either case, all guests should receive the same (or same kind) of invitation, even your closest friends.

Whatever the style, the most important aspect of an invitation is clarity. Tell invitees *who* is inviting them *where* and *when*, and exactly *what* to expect: Will there be a buffet supper? Cocktails and hors d'oeuvre? A barbecue? Although your party may not be formal enough to dictate dress, you still want to give people a sense of what to wear. Guests who show up expecting a casual buffet will be underdressed for a formal seated dinner, and the reverse is also uncomfortably true.

In order to help convey the mood, you can also explain *why* you're giving a party (especially when there is a birthday or anniversary involved), and most certainly use the invitation to indicate anything special guests should do, like don a costume, write a limerick, or keep a secret. If you are inviting people who have never been to your home, include a map and a set of written directions.

Guest Count Guidelines

Protocol prescribes that an invitation to the White House from the President is a command performance that cannot be refused. But since that's not the case in your own home, any written invitation that you issue should include a reply request line specifying the need for a response. Although the R.S.V.P. (a request for confirmation whether or not the guest will be attending, from the French phrase *respondez s'il vous plait* for "please respond") means more work for the host, it remains the safest way to record an accurate guest count. If you send an invitation bearing the request "Regrets only" (requiring a response only if the guest cannot attend), the invitation can get placed on the recipient's "to do" pile and may never be returned.

If you extend your invitation over the phone, always speak directly to the invitee, even if you plan on following up with a note. It spares everyone the embarrassment of missed messages. As your party draws near and you begin to tally your list, it is perfectly acceptable to telephone any guest whose attendance is in question, particularly since you may need to finalize arrangements with your caterer.

Comfort and Atmosphere

NO MATTER HOW MUCH HELP YOU'VE RECEIVED from professionals, never let your party acquire that hard veneer of perfection. Contrived, everything-just-so preparations can make the most beautifully decorated rooms seem too studied and museum-like. Finished with his embellishments, celebrated interior designer Billy Baldwin instructed clients,

"All right. Now mess it up." The same canon holds true for home entertaining: Precision is not as important as personality. Even when you must reduce clutter on tabletops for extra space at larger gatherings, don't hide away the jumble of your family's life. "It's not the houses I've loved, it's the life I've led in them," confessed style icon Coco Chanel. This sort of appealing intimacy makes a home warm and welcoming, even on the most formal occasions.

Smoke Screens

"Even though people can get so crazy about smoking these days, I don't restrict it," says Adrienne Vittadini. She puts ashtrays out, uses Rigaud candles (which help take the smoke scent out of a room), and thinks that most smokers understand they must be discreet.

Suzanne Williamson has another solution. "Since we live in the South and have lots of porches, people tend to congregate outside when they want to smoke. But if someone is a nonstop smoker, and I am especially fond of that particular person, I don't say a word if they smoke in the house. I just open the windows after the party to let in the air."

First, tend to the specifics of making your guests comfortable: keep them cool. Nothing stifles a party's spirit like overheated rooms. During the winter, turn thermostats down to 65°F several hours before guests are due. Rooms that feel cold to you will heat up as they fill up. In hot weather, prechill your rooms with full-blast air-conditioning, keeping the kitchen door closed and exhaust fan on to dissipate cooking heat and odors. All closed (and otherwise visible) windows should be clean and free of streaks. Remember, light (natural or not) can add to a room's temperature, so keep shades lowered and lamps off until the last possible moment. Resist the temptation to overperfume your house with environmental fragrance like incense, potpourri, scented candles, or room sprays, no matter how organic. The best way for a house to smell is fresh; keep your rooms well ventilated.

Plan ahead to create the environment you want before guests arrive. Fussing and making adjustments during a party gives guests a distracting glimpse into the machinery that sets your party in motion and makes them uncomfortable. Keep the guest bathrooms free of clutter and softly lit, with fresh soap, a small bottle of hand lotion, and hand towels available. Extra supplies (more towels, toilet paper, and tissues) should be visible but not obtrusive.

Flowers

W HEN IT COMES TO DECORATING YOUR HOME for a party, the days of relying on a florist can be over—if you want them to be. Upscale "bucket shops" and flower stalls in gourmet supermarkets sell everything from the standard bunched flowers like tulips and roses to Dutch lilacs and ranunculus, exotic blooms once available only through florists. Even when you don't compose the arrangements (perhaps this is a task performed by household staff), you can still add a personal touch by selecting the flowers yourself. Before using cut flowers in any arrangement, re-cut the stems with a sharp knife (some experts argue this should be done under running water to keep stems from sealing) and crush woody stems to allow water to be absorbed.

Making Other Arrangements

Finding a floral decorator is another one of those service situations when you can benefit from word-of-mouth, and this time your caterer may be able to help. Since caterers work with different florists in different homes, they can often recommend someone whose style and personality complements your own. Before any interviews take place, save time by reviewing the florist's work. Since not all floral designers have a retail store, many (who may have only a work space) rely on a "book"—a picture portfolio of what they consider to be their best work. You might not find exactly what you're looking for, but leafing through the photographs will give you a sense of the florist's overall style. If you are interested in developing a working relationship, arrange a meeting in your home. Obviously the floral designer will be able to do some "homework" by taking note of your color scheme and general taste, but you can provide help by showing him or her the containers available for arrangements, all the configurations of your dining table (with and without extending leaves) and the linens you use when entertaining.

Do your research before you meet and be prepared to give specifics. Is the look you're after loose and abundant? Structured and minimalist? Use magazine photographs to help the floral designer understand exactly what you want, including the condition of the flowers. Do you like open blooms? Mixed buds and

blooms? Flowers with leaves still attached? Lay down your floral guidelines. You may not know the name of every flower you like, but you can probably name the ones you don't. And be adamant about avoiding overpowering scents.

To save bottlenecks when preparing for larger gatherings, advise floral designers that they must be gone before the caterer arrives, particularly when the flowers are being arranged in your home. If the flowers are being assembled elsewhere for drop-off service, make sure each arrangement will be clearly labeled as to where it goes, and that there are several extra stems of matching flowers, in case an arrangement needs a last-minute adjustment.

Less Can Be Just Enough

Whether you are using a floral designer or doing the flowers yourself, don't go overboard. Towering pedestal arrangements and out-of-proportion floral displays have an unfortunate reverse effect by making nature seem artificial. Save vertical arrangements for areas where they complement architecture, like the entrance hall, mantel, or any featured location where flowers might act as sculpture. A tall ginger jar of gracefully swaying French tulips dramatically illustrates that luxury is a flower that fades well.

A buffet table is the ideal place for that big centerpiece, even if you don't place it right in the center. But keep it simple: a porcelain or pottery tureen filled with lemons or oranges; a strategically placed herbal topiary; a silver vegetable dish (sans cover) holding whole seasonal vegetables. It is best to avoid any arrangement featuring food that is to be eaten as part of the meal, like a centerpiece made from bread.

Lighting

NOTHING REVEALS the impact lighting has on mood quite like the story behind the opening of Radio City Music Hall in 1932, when excited conversations about the spectacular Art Deco design in the huge, brightly lit lobby were so loud that they carried over into the adjacent theater, disturbing audiences. The simple solution to this problem came from an enlightened designer who realized that the brighter the bulbs, the bigger the voices. When lobby lights were dimmed to the lowest possible level—where they remain to this day—conversations became hushed and the show went on smoothly. It's easy to apply this theory to the overall lighting scheme for your own party by keeping lights brighter during cocktails when conversation is the main event, and softer when the curtain goes up in the dining area.

Luminaries

To create a welcoming and comfortable party atmosphere in your dining area, you need a combination of diffused and focused light. Overhead lighting (from recessed or pendant fixtures) can be unflattering and is effective only when it is flexible, with adaptable intensity that can be regulated by a programmable lighting panel or dimmer switches. There's no need for "task lighting" (single notes of brightness) in the dining room, not unless you expect your guests to do needlepoint while they eat. What you want to achieve is "kind light"; the sort that keeps everyone looking their best, feeling relaxed, and happily engrossed in good conversation—just what producer, director, and screenwriter Joseph Mankiewicz must have had in mind when he described a Hollywood event as "two hundred and seventeen minutes of high thought and low lighting."

Dimmer switches are also helpful in entryways, hallways, and on staircases and landings—anywhere you want to shed a little light on a guest's ability to navigate without creating the linear light path of an airport runway. In other rooms, ambient lighting is best provided by well-placed table lamps and torchières that create soft pools of light exactly where you want them. The quality of lamp light can be adjusted by experimenting with bulbs of varying wattage and color (think pink!) as well as lampshades. Although lamps can never re-create the subtle shifts of natural light that blend light with shadow and shade, electric light diffused through texture is always interesting; lampshades do this, and they cast distinctive shadows as well.

Divine Light

Whoever said "The best way to light your home for a party is with a match" wasn't a pyromaniac. These were probably the words of a caterer who understood the seductive pull of kinetic lighting (from moving sources like fire and candlelight), and its power to draw people into the nooks and crannies of any room, putting odd space to good use at larger gatherings and creating intimate conversational groups. With the added attraction of a working fireplace, you can offer guests both hearth and home. But as romantic as gathering your guests around a roaring fire can be, bear in mind that leaping flames throw off

Flameproof

Always burn candles with safety in mind. Buy candles that fit securely in their holders. Never shave a candle (if it is too thick) or wrap anything around the base (if it is too thin). Place candle adhesive (available in press-on "dots") in the bottom of holders to keep tapers from toppling, and use bobeches (glass collars that slide down to the point where the taper meets the holder) to prevent dripping wax from ruining a table or linens. Votive candles, meant to liquefy in order to give long-lasting light, should be burned in holders not much larger than they are.

Keep all types of candles at least ten inches away from vents, open windows (or any other source of a possible breeze), lampshades, and any flammable objects. Trimming wicks to a quarter of an inch will keep candles from smoking and prevent flare-ups. No matter how beautiful the effect, never arrange candles where they can be easily jostled, a particular hazard at larger gatherings, and always extinguish flames when candles burn down to within two inches of holders. Candles should not be left unattended; light table candles in the dining room at the last moment, extinguishing any left burning in other rooms while the guests are being seated.

152

radiant heat. Position wood in the back of the firebox, keep fires small and protective screens in place.

Although you can count on firelight to cast a relaxing glow at any time of the day, candles should be lit only after dark (for safety tips, see "Flameproof," opposite page). Vibrantly colored and novelty candles may look festive during the holidays, but candlelight reflected through a natural palette (ivory whites and ivory yellows or the honey tones of beeswax) casts a more luminous glow during the rest of the entertaining year. Rely on classic shapes: pillars (of varying heights and dimensions, with or without protective hurricane shades) including cathedral candles (pillars in glass cylinders), tapers (ranging from six to eighteen inches in height), or votive candles.

Place subtly scented candles in the entrance hall and guest bathrooms, but never in the dining area or rooms where cocktails are being served. Light scented candles thirty minutes before guests arrive and store them covered, away from direct sunlight or excessive heat, at the party's end. On dining tables, candlelight kept below eye level casts the most flattering light (the real reason why votives are so popular in romantic restaurants). Using candles en masse (especially the same color, in varying shapes and heights) adds drama to any room. So do votive candles placed along the windowsill of bare, closed windows, where their twinkling light is reflected on both sides of the glass.

Music

ANYONE WHO HAS EVER CRINGED OR CRIED on cue at a movie knows the power of a music sound track. Your party can benefit from the same kind of careful scoring. However, with apologies to aficionados for whom music is never incidental, laying down a seamless blanket of sound under (not over) a party means avoiding selections with too much personality that might distract or overwhelm your guests: bouncy show tunes, improvisational jazz, soaring arias. Even an old-fashioned orchestral score can be too dramatic. But since you can go to the other extreme and lull your guests into boredom with monotonous New Age or "elevator music," experiment until you develop an effective party repertoire.

Go with the Flow

The right kind of music at the right volume weaves a subliminal structure that can set, adjust, or maintain the pace of any party, bridging those awkward gaps when a conversation falls a little short of fabulous. Start by dividing the party

up musically. For example, a seated dinner: the cocktail hour calls for the musical equivalent of the tinkle of ice cubes, something nonchalant like the cool sway of a bossa nova from time-tested masters Joao Gilberto and Antonio Carlos Jobim. It is generally a good idea to stay away from vocal music during dinner. No matter how well-adjusted the volume, there will come a time when guests may have to compete with the singing. Instead, rely on lyrical classical music to underscore an elegant ambience, one best described by critic Malcolm Bradbury as "sweetness and light and plenty of Mozart." Wind down your party with smooth jazz, from Chet Baker, perhaps, or the smoky vocals of Diana Krall. You can also have a little more fun with the music you play during coffee and dessert in the living room. Even the most devoted Sinatra fans will enjoy the same standards sung by offbeat vocalists like Fred Astaire, Johnny Hartman, or Joe Williams.

Although it may take a little trial and error to find just the right recording, you don't have to be an ethnomusicologist to appreciate the global beat of "world music." Perhaps it was the influence of fusion food, but savvy restaurateurs can take credit for establishing Afro-Caribbean rhythms, Latin-tinged Cape Verdian music, and ultra-romantic hybrid flamenco as sophisticated sound tracks for dining. Start a world beat tour by asking your favorite maître d' for recommendations, try one of the many crossover compilations or rely on surefire international superstars like Brazil's Caetano Veloso.

Since the average playing time of a CD is forty-five minutes (and your CD player may hold several at one time), labeling the cover of your favorites with precise times will help you calculate the length of your selections. Presort CDs for your particular party needs. For example, a seated dinner party requires at least two CDs for cocktails (about an hour and a half), three for the dinner portion of the evening (about two hours), and two more for coffee and conversation following the meal.

The Bar

NEXT TO DESIGNING A MENU, another challenge a host faces is deciding what bar beverages to serve. While restaurants pride themselves on the scope of their bars and stock a vast array of spirits that can be combined into numerous elaborate concoctions, home bars fall into three more realistic categories: wine and beer (for casual parties and/or large gatherings like an open house); modified-full (wine and beer augmented with vodka, gin, scotch, and traditional mixers like soda and tonic); and the full bar (a modified bar augmented with bourbon, tequila, rum, rye or blended whiskey, half bottles of sweet and dry vermouth, a full range of soda mixers plus orange, cranberry, grapefruit, and seasoned tomato juice). Every home bar starts with flat and sparkling water, regular and diet cola, and lemons and limes. Add cocktail olives and onions to the list when planning for a full bar.

Although there will always be a drink of the moment, serving one classic cocktail (like martinis or Manhattans) can become your entertaining trademark. So can offering a single "theme" drink designed to match your menu: margaritas with Southwestern dishes, or rum-laced *mojitos* for food with a Latin flavor. For those who prefer small dinner parties, it's nice to have an aperitif like Campari as a prelude to the meal and several after-dinner drinks (also called digestives) like port and cognac on hand. One hard-and-fast rule applies to the home bar: Yes, the larger the party, the simpler the bar can be. But if your invitation beckons guests for "cocktails," then you must offer them mixed drinks, regardless of the party's size (see Chapter Three).

Drinks from home bars are served in two ways: tray service (a butler takes the guest's order and delivers the drink or circulates with a tray bearing

How Much is Enough?

156 **Running out of bar supplies is one way a party can go off track. Here are rules of thumb for calculating amounts of all the basics (when in doubt, overestimate).**

Drinks

First the disclaimer: Drinking is a very regional, very personal thing. And no one knows your guests like you do. That said, here's a "guest-estimate": one 750-milliliter bottle of wine will pour four to six glasses; a 750-milliliter bottle of spirits makes about sixteen drinks. Although a caterer may give suggestions about what to serve, ordering spirits, wine, and other bar beverages is usually left to the host. To assort your exact selections, ask the salesman at your liquor store. They are usually good at converting the number of guests and length of a party into a formula for buying wines and spirits, including overages. They can also explain the store policy on returning what you do not use. Buy wine, water, and soda by the case, and always more than you think you'll need. They store well.

Ice

You will need about two pounds of ice cubes per person, almost three during warmer months. (Yes, really.) Commercial ice is typically sold in "party tubs"—lidded plastic containers with sturdy handles for easy transport—that hold about thirty-five

pounds of perfectly made cubes. You can also purchase crushed ice for chilling wine or beer, sold in thirty-pound bags (one bag will fill a standard rental icing tub and chill a full case of either).

Glasses

For a seated dinner, allow two glasses per person during the cocktail hour plus the glasses needed at each place setting (usually water, red and white wine, depending on what is being served). At a two-hour cocktail party or open house, allow three glasses per person. This does not mean your guests will drink three cocktails. It means that when they ask for a glass of water, there will be something to put it in. Do whatever you can to prevent rewashing—nothing is worse than a cold, fresh drink in a hot, wet glass.

Cocktail Napkins

Cloth is best for formal dinners, while paper is fine for larger gatherings. Plan on three paper napkins per guest for drinks and triple that number when hors d'oeuvre are being served. No matter how irresistibly priced, avoid rough, supermarket-quality paper cocktail napkins. Softer, more absorbent napkins can be purchased at a party goods shop or included in a rental order.

prepoured glasses of wine and water), and the stationary bar (guests walk up and order drinks from a bartender). Combining both of these methods facilitates service at large gatherings, ensuring that no one is empty-handed unless he or she wants to be.

Ice

Fact of life: Parties are notoriously ice and glass intensive. Don't underestimate how much and how many you're going to need (see "How Much is Enough?," opposite page). Ice doesn't just chill a drink, it melts and becomes part of the drink, like any other flavoring agent. (Ice melts more slowly and drinks stay colder when mixers like soda and juices are prechilled.) No matter how big your freezer is, homemade ice absorbs odors from other foods being stored and can taste "off." Commercial ice is frozen to stay individually cubed—meaning it doesn't "clump" like ice sold in the freezer case at supermarkets. Guaranteed to be flavor-free, commercial ice is sold at old-fashioned ice houses and large liquor stores or beer distributors. Be prepared: Most ice houses deliver COD. No checks, no credit cards.

Glasses

If the small dinner party is your favorite entertaining style, the best glasses to stock are: wine (a big, open, sphere-shaped red-wine glass along with a slimmer tulip glass for white wine, or a medium-sized glass that can be used for both); champagne (tulip and flute, both shaped to allow bubbles to rise, or the saucer-shaped *coupe*, supposedly modeled on one of Marie Antoinette's breasts); a few basic cocktail glasses like a highball or Collins glass for mixed drinks, soda, or water; and a whiskey or old-fashioned glass for drinks on the rocks. You can add a specialty glass, like a martini glass, footed beer Pilsner, or cordial glass, depending on your drink preferences.

For larger parties it is more economical (in terms of money and space) to use one versatile stemmed glass (about a ten-ounce capacity) for both wine and mixed drinks, available in quantity at restaurant supply companies or through a party rental company (see Rentals, page 158). Besides its machine-made durability, the all-purpose stemmed glass has another advantage: It won't drip like a tall, straight-sided glass will, so it is easier for guests to hold.

Bar Accessories

At large gatherings, bartenders don't want to fumble around with small bar equipment like jiggers, shakers, and strainers. They don't have time to refill an ice bucket, preferring to scoop the ice right out of the party tub (tongs are out of the question). As a result, you need very little fancy bar equipment. Here's what catering bartenders want you to supply: a small plastic cutting board and a small sharp knife (for cutting lemons and limes), a sharp vegetable peeler (for lemon twists, although some bartenders will use a knife), and several large ice scoops. Bartenders also appreciate a stack of clean side towels or oversized cloth napkins (both in white only) and inexpensive pitchers for juices—nothing they have to worry about breaking when the party picks up speed. A corkscrew is considered part of a catering staff person's uniform, and most professionals use a professional weight "waiter's tool." This sturdy compact combination, which folds up like a pocket knife, includes a two-and-a-half-inch screw (called a worm) for long corks, and a bottle opener. It never hurts to have one of your own.

Rentals

IT MAY SOUND TOO GOOD TO BE TRUE: all the equipment you need for entertaining delivered pristine and party-ready and then picked up without so much as a quick rinse. But that's the role rental companies play in the grand scheme of party things. Although they stock a variety of glassware and table settings, rental companies excel at supplying utilitarian items that make an unglamorous but invaluable contribution to any party: industrial trash cans (for easier clean-up and recycling); icing tubs (for chilling wine, beer, and champagne); bar mats and no-slip plastic runners (to protect the floor under bars and in the kitchen); oversized coffeemakers; heavy-duty coat racks and wooden hangers.

Most caterers work closely with a rental company and consider it part of their job to compile and call in your list of equipment needs. Rental companies will deliver the same day of the party (or the day before, if you are hosting a luncheon) and pick up the day following the party. It is standard policy to deliver COD, although many rental companies will take a credit card number over the telephone. If you decide to compile your rental list and call it in to the rental company, don't do it alone. Rely on the expertise of the rental company representative for table sizes and quantities of stemware, flatware, and china, as well as providing a reminder for things you may not even know you need.

Place Settings

The decision to rent china, flatware, and glasses depends on the number of guests, not the number of place settings you have in your china closet. Rental

equipment is simply more practical for a crowd. Since everything can be returned without being washed, clean-up time is cut in half, which can eliminate overtime charges from a staff who may already be keeping you up past your bedtime.

A good rule of thumb is to use your own china, glassware, and flatware for seated parties and rental equipment for buffets, where the party drifts into several rooms. Motion means action, and action can mean breakage; rentals minimize that trauma. However, make it a practice to rent glasses for larger parties. Glasses are the items most often broken (by guests, not staff), and you need plenty (see "How Much Is Enough?," page 156).

For home use, rental companies typically offer three levels of china: clear glass (the least expensive, these have a tendency to scratch with use, limiting them to the most casual outdoor parties); classic wedding band–style china (white with silver rim or ivory with gold—a very safe choice); or solid white china (from unadorned, everyday coupe-style plates to better-quality porcelain with a decorative rim).

Flatware, available in stainless or silver-plate, has a similar range, from the traditionally sized and weighted to the new larger and heavier bistro style. Not all flatware patterns include every utensil. But if you have reached the point where your entertaining style demands a fish fork, it's time to invest in your own silver.

When it comes to china and flatware, it is never a good idea to mix rental and in-house tableware, even if you're only a few place settings short. There's always a chance that during the confusion of the party clean-up something of yours will go back with the rentals, and it will be almost impossible to retrieve.

Linens

Even when you must rent china and flatware, it's always nice to use your own linens. Most rented linens are made of blended fiber in an institutional weight and can be coarse to the touch. In addition, rental cloths are cut to fit standard-size rental tables and will never provide the right "hang" on your own dining room table.

For versatility on the table, buying a selection of linens is the best party investment you can make—it's certainly more cost- and space-effective than owning and storing many sets of dishes. Tablecloths will instantly change the color and texture of your table. Place mats, available in varying shapes and sizes, and narrow, decorative runners, usually placed along the center of a bare table, add a different style and highlight the tabletop as well. Since napkins are easy to carry

Full House

Party rental companies (see page 158) can supply everything you need to extend the number of people you are able to seat in your home. Opinions vary about exactly how many guests can comfortably sit around standard-sized rental tables, but the consensus is that a forty-eight-inch round table will seat six; a fifty-four-inch round seats eight; and a sixty-inch round, ten. Here are some other things to keep in mind when you place your rental order:

ε• The tops of rental tables are often scratched and gouged: potholes from parties past. If you ask, most rental companies will provide a thin sheet of foam, cut to fit the tables you order. This pad acts like a silence cloth (see "Underlying Beauty," page 30), reducing noise and providing a little "cushion" to give the tablecloth a thicker feel and smoother surface. If the rental company does not have foam sheets, a thin blanket (as long as the texture is smooth) or flannel-backed oilcloth can be placed over the surface of the rental table before the tablecloth is laid.

ε• Unlike the tablecloths you use on your own table (where an overhang of twelve to fifteen inches is long enough to be considered formal), cloths for rental tables must fall to the floor in order to cover their unattractive metal legs. If you have to rent undercloths (because they are specifically sized to fit rental table), use your own tablecloths over them.

ε• Full-service caterers often have a "swatch-book" (from a rental company with whom they do regular business) with color and fabric samples of the available tablecloths.

Choosing ecru or ivory cloths instead of harsh "rental white" will result in a softer, more natural look.

ε• Although some party rental companies offer decorative overlays (referred to as toppers), placing your own tablecloths (a smaller round or square) over solid color rental cloths adds textural interest, fresh color contrast, and a personal touch.

ε• Anyone who has wiggled into a chair at a cramped dinner party and felt trapped there for the remainder of the evening understands the importance of positioning a table. To calculate the space you need, add two and a half feet (on all sides) to the circumference of the table. This will allow each guest to sit comfortably and still provide a "service alley" for the staff.

ε• The two most popular styles of rental chairs are ballroom (sometimes called reception) and folding. While these chairs take up the same amount of space (each is about eighteen inches wide), they are not interchangeable. Ballroom chairs, with bamboo-patterned back and legs, are considered to be more formal, and most rental companies carry them in many colors other than the ubiquitous "gold." Some even stock the chairs in natural or stained wood. Ballroom chairs come with tie-on seat cushions, which can be ordered to match the table's undercloth or overlay. Larger rental companies (usually those specializing in galas and weddings) may also provide chair covers (ranging from chair backs to full slipcovers). Folding chairs, typically offered in white, black, or natural wood, are best suited to informal and outdoor parties.

and store, which makes them fun to collect when you travel, acquiring an impressive assortment doesn't take much thought and planning. Vary the patterns all you like, but stick with napkins in the same color family so they can be combined for large dinners and buffets.

How to Be a Host

I T'S NO EXAGGERATION to claim that you're "throwing a party"—entertaining requires action and energy . . . and not just from you. Truly great parties are the result of a winning collaboration. Sure, you may set the stage, but your guests fill it—some better than others. The one important quality shared by accomplished hosts and thoughtful guests is experience; parties come to life when everyone understands their particular entertaining roles.

You're Only as Good as Your Guests

Assembling a dynamic guest list is a host's most significant contribution to a party's success. Marvelous flowers, delicious food, just the right music: Nothing matters if you don't have a lively mix of guests, considered by the late Edna Woolman Chase, *Vogue*'s longest reigning editor-in-chief, to be the makings of a good "social salad." At work-related parties (or even when you feel you must repay social debts), why limit your party to people who are "all business"? The worst common denominator for any guest list is a sense of obligation. (And don't kid yourself, guests can feel it.)

You'll be a better host (and have a better time) if you draw on people from different parts of your world, combining business associates, social acquaintances, and "paybacks" with intimates you can count on to be irresistibly charming. If you suffer from "balanced table syndrome" and worry about matching everyone to a partner, trust stage collaborators Edna Ferber and George Kaufman, who observed that guests are "invited for dining, not mating," in their witty play *Dinner at Eight*.

Work the Door

"The heartbeat of a house starts at the front door," announced Billy Baldwin, and that's never more true than at a party. When you are not answering the door yourself, assign a staff member to greet guests and take their coats. (A hanging mirror in the entrance hall so guests can take a quick look before entering the party is a lovely courtesy.) However, the most cordial greeting from a staff member does not substitute for a warm welcome from you. Don't wander too far from the front door; you don't want anyone to stand on the brink of entering the main room, even for a short time. Lingering in the doorway of a party can be the scariest twenty seconds of a shy guest's life.

Don't Send Rover Over

No matter how attached you are to your pets, assorted paws and stray hairs can make guests uncomfortable. Keep pets where they can't be seen *or* heard.

Making Introductions

A savvy host knows how to make introductions that include a little biographical information. "Alice, I'd like you to meet Martin" doesn't go anywhere. But "Alice, I'd like you to meet Martin—we worked together on the ballet benefit" can launch a conversation. It's also a good custom to maneuver new faces into groups that include old friends—those who can touch down on common conversational ground with just about anyone.

Controlling the Menu

As concerned as a host should be with the comfort of guests, when it comes to food you can't please everyone. If you are giving a party in someone's honor, by all means check with him or her so you can serve some favorite dishes. But trying to plan a menu around the likes and dislikes of your other guests will make entertaining impossible—there won't be anything left to serve. Considerate menu planning means selecting dishes that almost everyone can enjoy (easy on the exotica), that fit the formality of the occasion, and are easy to handle (no bones at buffets). At hors d'oeuvre parties and buffets, guests can choose from a variety of foods; at a butlered, plated meal, what guests choose to eat is up to them. A host should never monitor (or comment on) what is left on a guest's plate.

Plan Ahead, but Not too Much

Organize all you want, but the truth is that parties have a life of their own—when

you let them. If you yearn to be a good host, the real skill to cultivate is an ability to remain poised, no matter what happens. Time will teach you to risk it and relax. And as you learn to let your parties take their course, you will find that your guests can wind up somewhere even better than you planned.

What-a-Surprise Party

WITH ALL THE ADVANCES in communication technology, it's hard to believe that people still make unexpected drop-in visits. One knock and suddenly you're propelled across the divide between homebody and host. In the face of full-frontal drop-ins, take refuge in humorist P. G. Wodehouse's sensible rule and "never apologize" about anything, from the condition of your home to the state you're in.

You might be tempted to describe them in other ways, but drop-in guests can be summed up in two little words: "sweet" or "savory." With a few standard pantry items, you can easily accommodate either category. Although the crossover between sweets and savories usually occurs in the late afternoon, where you draw the line with drop-ins is completely up to you. Quickly assemble a tray, including small plates and napkins, and move your guests to the part of the house in which you feel most comfortable.

Off Guard, but Never Unprepared

For sweets: a thermal carafe of coffee or a pot of tea, served with Scottish shortbread or French butter biscuits. *For savories*: a simple white wine or aperitif (like Lillet Blanc or Rouge), salted nuts, plus herb or pepper crisps that taste great with or without cheese. It doesn't hurt to stock a few extra bottles of still and/or sparkling water; cola and/or diet cola (a perfect place for party leftovers). During the holidays, when drop-ins are more frequent, add a good hot chocolate and some seasonal cookies, or keep champagne and/or sparkling cider with an emergency pound cake in the refrigerator. The drop-in guest pantry is also a great place for all those gourmet impulse items you can't resist and never know when to serve.

How to Be a Guest

Be on Time

Whether your invitation comes through the mail or over the telephone, a prompt response is the first sign of a good guest. The second is to show up when you're supposed to. Your invitation will tell you what time to arrive and that's exactly when your host expects to see you. Ten minutes late may be acceptable, but ten minutes in the other direction just won't work. There are many last-minute adjustments taking place right before the guests arrive, and in most cases, the early bird actually becomes the worm.

Don't Bring Anything or Anyone

When you are formally invited to someone's home, rest assured that they have already planned and paid for everything they need, including wine, dessert, and, most of all, flowers. Taking an expensive vase from its hard-to-reach storage cupboard in a kitchen where every inch of space is being used makes cutting and arranging a bunch of flowers more than a chore, it's an imposition. If you insist on believing that myth about not arriving empty-handed, a box of hand-packed boutique chocolates requires no maintenance and is still considered a luxury, regardless of income bracket.

Unless it specifically states that you may bring a guest, your invitation is for you alone. Never assume otherwise, and this is particularly true where your children are concerned. No matter how informal a party may seem, your host may have a child-free environment in mind.

Engage

At larger gatherings where you are set loose to mingle on your own, always include a short identifying phrase when you introduce yourself, something that might reveal a shared interest. And remember that being a good conversationalist consists of talking *and* listening, even when you think you're the most fascinating person in the room.

Special Orders Do Upset Hosts

Legitimate food imperatives (like an allergy or religious restrictions) are the host's concern. Briefly explain them when you accept an invitation. Food issues of your own choosing (say you're a vegetarian or finicky about carbohydrates) are your own problem. Keep them to yourself.

Make a Graceful and Timely Exit

Your hosts will give you a hint when it's time to leave. At a formal dinner party, listen for the phrase "coffee in the living room." It means that you are entering the final stage of the evening. At cocktail parties, it's time to leave when your hosts station themselves near the door. They want you to use it.

Give Thanks

Always send a handwritten note that includes some special detail about the party. But depending on the nature of your relationship with the hosts (and the frequency of your guest appearances), you may also choose to send small personal gifts, like books or music you know they will enjoy. In formal situations, flowers may be a more appropriate gift. Unless you have a florist with whom you do regular business, be specific about the style of the flowers when you order. You don't thank a host for a four-star meal in elegant surroundings with a standard arrangement that screams McFlowers.

Acknowledgments

IT ISN'T OFTEN I get to officially thank the people who have helped me along my way, and I am balanced between boring you senseless and consolidating my list in order to keep your attention because I have been so very lucky, and here's why.

When I came to New York City in 1981, Sheila Lukins gave me a job as the catering director of the Silver Palate. And as if that weren't enough, I got to work alongside Bob Fabrizak, Joe Caselli, and Michael McLaughlin (who have all gone on to a greater reward) and Tom Viola and Lawrence Bender (who have both gone on to greater careers). These people meant the world to me.

In 1983, I opened my own catering business, and among my early clients I would like to thank Jon Tisch and his sister Laurie Tisch Sussman, Brooke and Andy Berger, Dena Kaye, and Nancy Fisher and Marc Kirschner. And later, it was also my privilege to cook in the homes of Jonathan and Joanna Coles and Myrna and Steve Greenberg. During my catering years, I worked with great people—my friends—and I would like to thank Dan Smith, Jessica Brieden, Susan Carragher, Cassandra Begos, Jan Fort, Faye Fayerman, Charles Mohacey, and Joe McLaughlin.

At different points in my career, I fell under the influence of three people: Pamela Fiori, Marcia Warner, and Lee Bailey. I can't remember exactly when I met each; they have combined into one glowing force in my mind. But I am what I am because they are who they are.

When I switched from catering to writing, it was because Nancy Evans told me to do it and Jann Wenner gave me the place to do it. Early on, I worked with Jim Brosseau at *Town & Country* who set the editorial bar extremely high, and then Tom Farley (*Town & Country*) and Wendy Israel (*Family Life*), who cleared it. I would also like to thank Tony Freund (*Town & Country*) and Brenda Vaughan (*Esquire*) for their consistent editorial direction as well as *Esquire* editor-in-chief David Granger for being plenty of fun to talk to. My gratitude and admiration goes to Jay Woodruff, my former *Esquire* editor, who gave me a once-in-a-lifetime assignment that in turn gave me a much different career than most people expected.

For their advice and support and the pleasure of viewing/reading their work, I would like to thank my colleagues (and friends) Andrew French, Henry Alford, Justin Spring, Steven Jenkins, and David Carr.

A writer needs friends; I have many. For the movies and the meals and the noodles around town, I would like to single out Randy Neff, Priscilla Warner, George Proschnick, Wayne Gryk, Sarah Woodruff, David Shannon Parker, Anthony Gentile, Suzanne Williamson, Steve Brown, Kevin Hills, and Mitch Gruner. I would also like to thank my brother Tom and his wife Carol for doing all the driving.

It doesn't take a brilliant genius to figure out that I didn't make this book happen alone: It took *Town & Country*'s Glenna MacGrotty (as the gatekeeper), Susan Wechsler of Fair Street Productions, and Jennifer Sanfilippo of Photosearch, Inc., as well as Clark Wakabayashi and Gregory Wakabayashi of Welcome Enterprises, Inc. But most of all, it took the fine editorial hand of Betty Rice.

I would love to thank my agent, Laura Blake Peterson, and her assistant, Kelly Going, for everything they do and how well they do it, but I'm afraid there isn't room. So I will sum it up quickly: *the best*. And thank you to the rest of the staff at Curtis Brown Literary; it is good knowing you are only a telephone call away.

And finally, I would like to thank my parents, Marty and Maddie, for providing the balance as well as the checks that have always encouraged my behavior.

Francine Maroukian
New York City, September 2003

Picture Credits

50	Marc Royce
52	Nadine Froger
53–55	Photograph © Julie Skarratt Photography Inc.
	Catering by Callahan Catering
56–57	Courtesy of Lynn and Oscar Wyatt, Jr.
59	Photograph by © Julie Skarratt Photography Inc.
	Flowers by Tansey Design Associates
60	Anita Calero
62–63	Nadine Froger
64	Thayer Allyson Gowdy, www.thayerphoto.com
66–69	Marc Royce
70	Photograph © Meg Smith,
	www.megsmith.com.Catering by Elaine Bell, CA
72	The Kobal Collection/MGM
73	The Kobal Collection/Paramount
75	Photograph by Michael Mundy
	Cake by Sylvia Weinstock
76–78	Michael Mundy
80–81	Oberto Gili
83	Photograph © Meg Smith, www.megsmith.com
	Event by Sasha Souza Design, CA
	Catering by Alex's Catering, CA
84, 86	Thayer Allyson Gowdy, www.thayerphoto.com
88	Newsmakers/ Getty Images
89	Courtesy of Cathleen Black, Hearst Magazines
91–93	Laura Resen
94	Thayer Allyson Gowdy, www.thayerphoto.com
95	Fernando Bengoechea/GM
96–97	Thayer Allyson Gowdy, www.thayerphoto.com
99–100	Courtesy of Mimi and John Bowen
	Photograph by Grevy Photography, New Orleans
103	Maura McEvoy
104	Photograph © Meg Smith, www.megsmith.com
	Event by Kristi Amoroso, CA
105	Thayer Allyson Gowdy, www.thayerphoto.com
106–07	Courtesy of Mimi and John Bowen
	Photograph by Grevy Photography, New Orleans
108	Photograph © Meg Smith, www.megsmith.com
	Event by Jeffrey Best, Best Events
110	Fernando Bengoechea/GM
112–15	Pamela Hanson
117	Marc Royce
118	Miki Duisterhof
119	T'Sas/Inside/Beateworks.com
120–21	Maura McEvoy
122	Courtesy of Patricia Cook
	Photograph © Lucien Capehart, Palm Beach
123	© Lucien Capehart, Palm Beach
125	Thayer Allyson Gowdy, www.thayerphoto.com
126–27	Miki Duisterhof
128	Petrina Tinslay
129	Photograph © Meg Smith, www.megsmith.com
	Event by Kristi Amoroso, CA
	Flowers by Ariella Chezar
130–31	Photograph © Meg Smith, www.megsmith.com
	Flowers by Tesoro, CA
	Catering by Wine Valley Catering, CA
133	Photograph © Meg Smith, www.megsmith.com
	Event by Kristi Amoroso, CA
	Catering by Carter Brown
137	Courtesy of Tansey Design Associates
	Photograph © Julie Skarratt Photography Inc.
139	Marc Royce
140–41	Nadine Froger
142	Michael Mundy
146–47	Photograph © Meg Smith, www.megsmith.com
	Event by Monica Pallie
149	Courtesy of Preston Bailey Designs,
	www.prestonbailey.com
	Photograph by John Labbe
151	Oberto Gili
154	Thayer Allyson Gowdy, www.thayerphoto.com
159	Courtesy of Tansey Design Associates
	Photograph © Julie Skarratt Photography Inc.
163	Petrina Tinslay
164–65	Stephanie Diani
166	Photograph © Julie Skarratt Photography Inc.
	Catering by Callahan Catering
169	© Meg Smith, www.megsmith.com
170–71	Courtesy of Tansey Design Associates
	Photograph © Julie Skarratt Photography Inc.

The producers gratefully acknowledge the cooperation of the all the people who supplied photographs for this book. We would also like to thank Pamela Fiori, Mary Shanahan, Michael Cannon, Casey Tierney, Mara Hoberman, and Glenna MacGrotty at Town & Country for their assistance.

Copyright © 2003 by Hearst Communications, Inc.

Produced by Welcome Enterprises, Inc. and Fair Street Productions

H. Clark Wakabayashi and Susan Wechsler, *Project Directors*
Gregory Wakabayashi, *Designer*
Jennifer Sanfilippo/Photosearch, Inc., *Photo Editor*

Library of Congress Cataloging-in-Publication Data

Maroukian, Francine.
  Town & Country elegant entertaining / Francine Maroukian.
p. cm.
"A Fair Street/Welcome Book."
  ISBN 1-58816-009-2
  1. Entertaining. 2. Cookery. I. Title: Town and Country elegant entertaining. II. Title.
TX731.M379 2003
642'.4--dc21

                    2003002278

                    1 3 5 7 9 10 8 6 4 2

Published by Hearst Books
A Division of Sterling Publishing Co., Inc.
387 Park Avenue South, New York, NY 10016

Town & Country and Hearst Books are trademarks owned by
Hearst Magazines Property, Inc., in USA, and Hearst Communications, Inc., in Canada.

www.townandcountrymag.com

Distributed in Canada by Sterling Publishing
c/o Canadian Manda Group, One Atlantic Avenue, Suite 105
Toronto, Ontario, Canada M6K 3E7

Distributed in Australia by Capricorn Link (Australia) Pty. Ltd.
P. O. Box 704, Windsor, NSW 2756 Australia

Manufactured in China

1-58816-009-2